THE *New* JEWISH HISTORY

BOOK ONE

From Abraham to the Maccabees

THE PUBLICATION of this volume, *The New Jewish History,* was made possible by the establishment of a fund for the publication of Jewish religious school literature by the NATIONAL FEDERATION OF TEMPLE SISTERHOODS

BOOK ONE

THE *New* JEWISH HISTORY

From Abraham to the Maccabees

MAMIE G. GAMORAN

Illustrated by BRUNO FROST

THE *Union*
OF AMERICAN HEBREW CONGREGATIONS

New York, N. Y.

TO

MY THREE JUDITHS

EDITOR'S INTRODUCTION

The aim of *The New Jewish History* by Mamie G. Gamoran is chiefly threefold: to emphasize what is interesting and dramatic in the story of the Jewish people; to stress the achievements of Judaism, particularly in the areas of social, religious, and cultural values; and, in telling the story of Jewish persecution, which cannot be ignored, to accent the inner fortitude which made it possible for Jews and Judaism to survive, holding aloft our great Jewish ideals despite tragedy.

Above all, the author sought to keep in mind the desirability of creating positive attitudes on the part of our children. They are to be led to feel that the history of their people is an unfinished story in which they will participate; that it is dramatic and challenging, and that the Jewish people have made important contributions to the world and to the peoples in whose midst they lived. It is a record of continuous achievement in spite of many adverse circumstances in which our people found itself. The account is therefore given as a running story, to hold the interest of the child. The events are presented for their dramatic quality and for their record of significant Jewish achievement along cultural, ethical, and spiritual lines. To what extent the author has succeeded in fulfilling these aims, our readers will have to judge.

Teachers have often expressed the thought that little children can learn in school only through the story-telling, dramatizing method. When they grow older, they are ready to receive information, and when they grow still older and are in high school, they begin to reason. Hence, writers of textbooks for younger children have felt that they must take only emotional appeal into consideration. This division has long been abandoned. We now know that children feel, learn, and think at the same time. To be sure, the writer has to bear in mind the age group for which he is writing, but youngsters often surprise us by their thinking ability. It is not wise to underrate them.

Bearing this in mind, the author has sought to present the facts of Jewish history frankly, to teach our children that not everything of our past is known. Scientific students, particularly those at work in Bible lands, are making new discoveries continuously. This book presents some of these new discoveries as part of the Jewish story which ought to be known by the children and seeks to stress the idea that we have still much to learn about our own people. As the research of scholars and students of Biblical history continues we will learn more and more about our own past.

The author has also sought to give emphasis to our religious and spiritual ideals and to convey to the children, even in the intermediate grades, that Judaism has been evolving and growing throughout the ages. The ideas of God held by the Judges were not as developed as those taught by the Prophets. Yet it is clear that from the very earliest days our people was distinguished by a concern for the brotherhood of man and a belief in a God who was a great universal Spirit, the Father of all mankind.

A printed edition of the Activity Book has now been issued to accompany this text. It is hoped that teachers and principals will keep in touch with us and will communicate to us their ideas as to how this text, the first in the series of *The New Jewish History* and its Activity Book, may be made more helpful, more suitable to the needs of the children in the intermediate grades. Both author and editor will be grateful for such suggestions.

The Union of American Hebrew Congregations hopes that this book will meet the needs of our schools and will contribute to the development on the part of our children of an appreciation and understanding of the great spiritual ideals which are reflected throughout our history.

EMANUEL GAMORAN

ACKNOWLEDGMENTS

I wish to acknowledge my deep indebtedness to the Reading Committee of the Commission on Jewish Education, consisting of Rabbi Leon Fram, chairman of the Committee on Schools, Dr. Solomon B. Freehof, and Dr. Harry M. Orlinsky, for the many hours of reading which they gave to the manuscript and for the guidance which I received from their helpful comments.

Others who read the manuscript and offered numerous suggestions were Mr. Samuel Grand and Rabbi Eugene J. Lipman. I am happy to express my thanks to them for their assistance.

Considering the many complex problems confronting the writer of early Jewish history for children, it is not surprising that I could not at all times agree with the readers in the interpretation of some situations and events of the early Biblical period. I carefully considered the different interpretations offered and I know the book was improved by the thoughtful criticisms which were made on different points. It is important to state that the final responsibility for the presentation rests with me.

Mrs. William Stodt, teacher at the New Lincoln School in New York City, was most helpful. Her experience as a teacher in the fifth grade was an excellent check on story-interest and language.

To Mr. Ralph Davis is due the credit for the fine appearance and design of the book. He was assisted by Mrs. Julia Minor and Miss Sylvia Schiff, through whose hands the manuscript passed, submitted originally to the Commission as the work of "Betty Held." Mr. Bruno Frost, the artist, was patient through many discussions, and his illustrations add greatly to the dramatic quality of the book.

My final "thank you" is to the editor. The idea for a history with an emphasis on drama, achievement, and spiritual values was his for many years. His stimulation and his guidance made it possible for me to attempt so big a project. I assumed this undertaking not fully aware of the responsibility it entailed. More and more, as

I studied and wrote, did I realize what it means to bring the story of our people to Jewish children, particularly in the first book of history which they meet in their religious school.

If I have succeeded in helping to set our children soundly on the road of satisfactory identification with their religion and their people, I shall be more than gratified. I am glad to share with all those who took part in this endeavor the satisfaction of accomplishment.

M. G. G.

New York, April, 1953

CONTENTS

EDITOR'S INTRODUCTION   vii

ACKNOWLEDGMENTS   ix

READ THIS BEFORE YOU BEGIN THE BOOK   3

Unit 1   The Beginnings of the Jewish People   5
    1. OUR WONDERFUL BIBLE   7
    2. LONG, LONG AGO   12

Unit 2   How the Hebrews Became a Free People   21
    3. A NEW HOME   23
    4. OUT OF BONDAGE   31
    5. THE LAWS OF MOSES   38
    6. IN THE DESERT   44

Unit 3   Early Days in Canaan   49
    7. A PREVIEW OF CANAAN   51
    8. WITH STRENGTH AND COURAGE   59
    9. WHEN THE JUDGES JUDGED   67

Unit 4   A United People   75
    10. THE FIRST KING   77
    11. THE SHEPHERD BOY   85
    12. THE KINGDOM GROWS   91
    13. THE GLORIOUS YEARS   98

Unit 5   A Nation Divided   107

      14. THREE FATEFUL DAYS   109

      15. UNDER TWO FLAGS   114

      16. THE MEN WHO SHOWED THE WAY   120

Unit 6   The Kingdom of Israel   127

      17. TROUBLED TIMES   129

      18. THE WARNING   137

      19. A KINGDOM IS LOST   144

Unit 7   Great Ideas in a Small Land   149

      20. DAY BY DAY   151

      21. THE WISE PROPHET   160

      22. A BOOK THAT MADE HISTORY   171

      23. WHEN JUDAH FELL   179

Unit 8   Beginning Again   187

      24. THE CRUCIAL TEST   189

      25. REBUILDING THE LAND   197

      26. THE QUIET YEARS   209

Unit 9   The Brave Maccabees   217

      27. THE WORLD COMES IN   219

      28. REBELLION   229

      29. INDEPENDENCE   236

CHILDREN'S READING LIST   241

TEACHER'S BIBLIOGRAPHY   243

PRONOUNCING LIST   245

INDEX   247

THE *New* JEWISH HISTORY

BOOK ONE

From Abraham to the Maccabees

Read This
Before You Begin the Book

How old are you? Ten years old? Perhaps eleven? How far back can you remember? Maybe you remember going on a picnic with your mother and father, or the first movie you ever saw, or your first day at school. That's probably four or five years ago. Who is the oldest man you know? Your grandfather, I guess. He may be fifty-five, or sixty-five or even seventy-five years old.

Of course you know that the things your grandfather and your grandmother did in their lives have something to do with the way you live today. You are an American because they or their father and mother left Europe many years ago to come to America. Suppose they had never gone away from home or they had decided to go to Cuba or to Brazil. You would be talking French or Polish or Portuguese instead of English at home and in school. You would wear different clothes and eat different foods and play different games.

What your grandfather's grandfather did many years earlier also has something to do with how you live today. It's all like a long chain, linking one person to another. And what we are told a certain man did thousands of years ago has ever so much to do with the kind of life you lead today. His name was Abraham. You will hear about him later. He is one of many men and women whose names you have heard over and over

3

again. How they lived and what they meant to the world will be found in the pages of this book. We are going on a long journey together. We will visit country after country and hear stories of war and of peace, of cowardice and of courage, of defeat and of triumph.

Reading a book is like listening to someone speak whom you cannot answer. But I do not want you only to listen. You will talk about what you read with the other boys and girls in your class and with your teacher and your parents. You will want to know more about the events and people in this book than I have written. I will tell you where you can read about them in other books. I hope you will write stories and poems, and draw pictures and charts about the men and women, the ideas and the discoveries, the hopes and the accomplishments that you will read about.

Most important of all, you will know that though you study about what has happened before to other people in other lands, you are making yourself ready to live honestly and faithfully, as a Jew in America. And now let us begin.

Unit 1

The Beginnings of the Jewish People

You have surely read stories of the men and women in the Bible. Names like Abraham, Joseph, and Elijah are familiar to you. You may have thought of them as belonging to the world of fancy and of legend.

Try to think of them now as real people, who lived an everyday life, who ate and slept, who were happy and sad at different times. The stories about them and about many other men and women were collected and written down by men who first heard them from their fathers and their grandfathers. Later on, priests and writers called scribes began to keep written records of what was happening in their times. Religious poems and songs, letters, and inscriptions on stones and monuments also tell of days long gone by.

The first man we meet in our book is Abraham. The Bible says that God promised to "make of him a great nation," and that in him, "all the families of the earth" would be blessed.

This book tells about Abraham's descendants, how they lived, and what some of them did to bring a blessing to the families of the world. The early chapters take us back to the days of Abraham.

And the land lay before them

1. OUR WONDERFUL
BIBLE

WHEN a baby is born, we know the day, the hour, even the minute it is born. Is this true about a people or a nation? Sometimes it is. More often it is not. It all depends on how the people comes into being.

Sometimes it is at a definite exciting moment. This is true mostly of modern peoples whose history we can easily trace back for it began only a few hundred years ago. Other nations were born long ago. Their past is cloaked in the mystery of bygone days. These are the ancient peoples. We have heard stories of their beginnings, and from these stories we can build up part of their history—what they did long ago, who were their heroes, where they lived. Sometimes visitors to lands far away find stones and clay tablets with writing on them, or discover monuments with inscriptions carved on them. Then a scholar will study these writings and compare them with other inscriptions which he already knows how to read, and lo and behold, he may have learned some important facts about an ancient people!

On July 4, 1776, a little boy ran to a church in Philadelphia, calling to the sexton, "Ring, oh, ring for Liberty!" The Decla-

ration of Independence had just been accepted by the delegates from the Thirteen Colonies and the American nation
was born. What an exciting dramatic moment in history! That
is one time that we know exactly when a nation was born.

Many years later, in the Palace of Versailles, near Paris,
France, delegates of the great nations of the world signed an
agreement setting aside a certain area of land in which certain
people had lived for many years, and created a new state
called Czechoslovakia. Once again we know almost the exact
moment this nation came into being.

On November 29, 1947, the United Nations General Assembly, meeting in Flushing Meadows, New York, voted to
partition Palestine into a Jewish state and an Arab state. On
May 14, 1948, in Tel Aviv, Palestine, the State of Israel was
proclaimed. Was either of these dates the beginning of the
Jewish people? No. They were great moments in Jewish history, but you know that the Jewish people is one of the
ancient peoples of the world, and had its beginnings long ago,
in days gone by, in a land far away. We do not have an exact
day or moment when it began. To tell us of its early days, we
do have tales of other old peoples, stories and legends, inscriptions on ancient stones, and treasures of the past. Above all,
we have the Bible.

You may ask if the stories in the Bible tell what really happened so many years ago. We think they do. The Bible is a
book of great religious teachings, of fine poetry and of marvel-
ous stories, and it is also a record of events which happened to
the Jewish people. Lately we have learned about some very
important and interesting happenings which help to make this
clear. In the lands which used to be the ancient world of

Mesopotamia and Canaan and Egypt, groups of scholars called archeologists have been digging at the places where old cities existed. Wonderful discoveries have been made. Sometimes the workers have found ruins of more than one city on one spot. This would happen when a city had been invaded by an enemy and was burned or destroyed. Years later another city would be built over the first. Thus, there are layers of ruined cities one beneath another, and as the diggers go farther down, older and older cities are uncovered. In this way, parts of very old cities have been discovered and studied.

In the ruins, household articles, jewelry, and ornaments have been found. Bowls and cups of special shapes and sizes have been discovered, together with many broken pieces of pottery. The bits of pottery are called potsherds. The vessels of pottery and the potsherds can tell an important story. Though the vessels may be found in different places, scholars have learned that at certain periods in old world history, and in different areas, men made the same kind of pottery. The potsherds help to decide the date of the city that is being studied.

You will understand this by a simple example which comes from our own day. You know what plastics are. The first plastic was celluloid. You have seen many celluloid objects in your own home—combs, boxes, containers of all sorts. Objects of this kind have been made only since about 1870. If our civilization were being studied in years to come, and celluloid articles were found, the students would know that they were made after the year 1870. There was no celluloid in existence at an earlier date.

Or we can take another example. In your home, no doubt, there is a telephone. There is a dial on the telephone. You use it to get your number. Years ago telephones were built without dials. They had a plain surface. An operator called your number for you. The first dial phone was installed in Indiana, in 1892. The first dial phone in New York City was installed in 1922. Can you see how finding a dial phone would help a future historian to date other objects? It would all depend on where the dial phone was discovered.

In the ruined cities of long ago something else very valuable was found. Thousands of clay tablets were uncovered. These tablets were the books and letters of ancient times. The scholars who deciphered what was written on the tablets got very excited. For some of the stories they read told of happenings very much like the stories of the Bible. The names of men and cities on some of the tablets are like the names of the people and cities in the Bible. Some of the very laws and customs written about in the Bible, which had been hard to understand, became clear after the tablets were found and read.

These tablets were discovered about 1935, so we today know more about the days of our forefathers than people knew even fifty years ago. Even though the stories of the Bible were written down many centuries after they happened, we believe that they tell about real people and real happenings. The inscriptions, the clay tablets, and the ancient vessels and pottery that are being discovered help to prove this. So far the Bible, more than anything else, tells us what happened long, long ago. That is why the books of the Bible are so important to people who are studying the history of the Jewish people.

SOMETHING IMPORTANT TO KNOW

You are living in the year 1965 or later. That means 1,965 years after the year 1. Many important events happened before the year 1. For example, Abraham lived about 1,900 years before the year 1. From the year 1 to the present time is called the Common Era (era means a period of time). We use the initials C.E. for Common Era. The period before the year 1, counting backwards, is called Before the Common Era, B.C.E.

SOMETHING TO DO

You are an archeologist working in the year 2400 C.E. Your world is very different from our present world. Our history books and documents have been destroyed. You have found a penny, a nickle, and a dollar bill among some ruins. What would they tell you about the world of today and the country we live in? Write a short report for the chief of your expedition.

Using the initials C.E. or B.C.E. write down the year you were born.

About what year did Abraham live?

READINGS FOR TEACHERS

Unit I (CHAPTERS 1–2)

The Bible, Gen. 12:1–10, 13, 23.

The Other Side of the Jordan by Nelson Glueck, Chap. I.

The Jews, Vol. I, ed. by Louis Finkelstein, Chap. I by William F. Albright, pp. 3–6.

A History of the Jewish People by Max L. Margolis and Alexander Marx, Chap. I.

Westminster Historical Atlas to the Bible by G. F. Wright and F. V. Filson, pp. 23–26, 30.

What Mean These Stones? by M. Burrows, pp. 1–29.

Encyclopedia of Bible Life by Madeline S. and J. Lane Miller (for general reference).

The Jewish Kindergarten by Deborah Pessin and Temima Gezari, pp. 141–143 and other pages for special activities.

Israel in the Ancient Near East by Harry M. Orlinsky, Chap. I.

2. LONG, LONG AGO

FAR AWAY in western Asia is the vast Arabian desert. It is a large flat land. This desert is not like other deserts, dry and brown. It has some places where enough rain falls for grass and vegetation to grow. In these spots in the center of the land and in the south, people could live. When the rainy season had come and the grass was green, their flocks of sheep and goats had plenty to eat, and their families could have milk and cheese. Later on in the year it would be harder to find food for everyone.

There was another area, green and fertile and pleasant, even more inviting for men to settle in with their families and their flocks. If you look at the map and follow the edge of the desert, beginning at the south with Egypt, up along the coast to Canaan and north to Aram, then eastward and south again to the ancient land of Mesopotamia and the Persian Gulf, you will find it. This region is shaped like a half-moon or crescent. Today we call it the Fertile Crescent. Two rivers, the Tigris and the Euphrates, watered its plains on the east, while the wonderful River Nile made the soil of Egypt rich and fertile. In Canaan, the Jordan River ran from the north to the south of the land. From it flowed smaller streams or tributaries, making a valley well suited to settlement and agriculture. Other

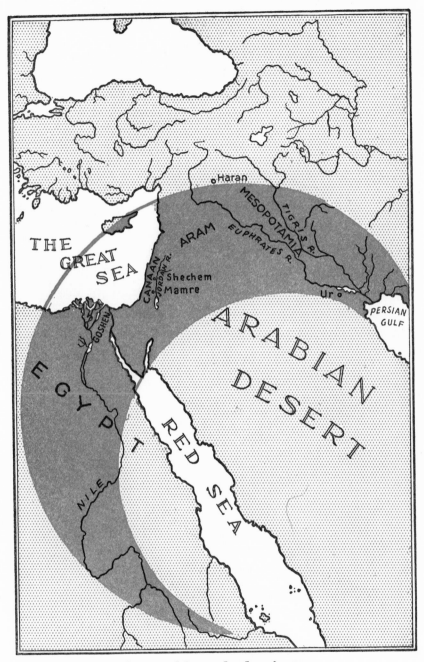

The World of Abraham's Day

fertile spots in the country were the Valley of Jezreel south of the Sea of Galilee, and the hill country of Judea, where the cities of Hebron and Jerusalem came to be located.

In these grasslands of Arabia and in the Fertile Crescent lived some of the ancient peoples of the world. The story of the Jewish people began here.

Again and again great waves of people came into the Fertile Crescent. From the north, over the mountains, came people who settled in cities and built up the kingdom of Babylonia. Here kings and nobles reigned in splendid palaces, and huge temples rose for the worship of many gods. From the desert in the south came wandering bands of shepherds, seeking the good lands of the Fertile Crescent for their flocks. These wanderers or nomads passed by the comfortable towns of Mesopotamia and the great cities of Egypt. They were not happy closed up in cities, surrounded by walls. They loved the open spaces, the nights spent under the stars, and their simple way of life, tending their flocks of sheep and goats. If they were not satisfied with one place, they could easily pick up their tents and move to a spot where the grass was more plentiful and where water could more easily be found.

Our ancestors were wandering shepherds of this kind. Their stories are in the Bible. From those ancient pages, a name leaps out at us. It is Abraham, the Hebrew, the Father of the Jewish People. Now we go back, back, almost thirty-nine hundred years to about the year 1900 B.C.E. Like so many other wanderers of this time, we are in Mesopotamia moving westward from the River Euphrates toward the River Jordan in Canaan. We find ourselves with Abraham and his family, part of a large caravan of men, women and children.

The tinkle of tiny bells mingles with the soft thud of the heavy broad feet of the camels as the caravan slowly winds across the desert sands. Donkeys, smaller but strong and wiry, move along more slowly, for they are heavily laden with household goods. The afternoon sun, still hot, shines down on the group. Sandaled children run alongside of the animals. Shepherds and goatherds walk in the rear among the sheep and the goats. All is quiet and peaceful. Everything seems to be in order. The caravan has confidence in its leader, Abraham. They know that he will find a good land for them, a country where there will be pasture for their flocks, place to set up their tents, and water for all.

All these men, women and children were really not Abraham's family. His own family was made up only of himself, his wife, Sarah, and his nephew, Lot. In those days a man's family, his servants, his shepherds, their wives, and their children were a united group. Such a group of families was called a clan. If the clan became very large, with many families, it was usually called a tribe. When we meet Abraham, moving with his caravan across the desert, he was the head of a tribe who called him Father. Abraham and his son, Isaac, and his grandson, Jacob, are called the three Patriarchs or Fathers.

This was not the first time that Abraham was on the march. He was born in Mesopotamia, in the town Ur of Chaldees, and there he lived for many years until his father went with his family north to the city of Haran. Now Abraham was leaving his brothers in Haran and was moving on. He was seeking a good place for his tribe to settle, a land where there would be fine pasture for his flock and plenty of room for them to move around.

The Bible gives a special reason for Abraham's journey. It connects his wanderings with his place in history, as the ancestor of the Jewish people. To understand this reason, we must know a little more about the people of Abraham's time.

In all the places that Abraham had dwelt, in Ur of Chaldees where he had lived as a boy, in Haran where he had grown to be rich and respected, all his friends, even his father, worshipped many gods. There were household gods and temple gods, gods of the field and gods of the city. People made wooden or stone images of these different gods and set them up in their homes and in the temples. These images are called idols. Each god had a special purpose. The household god was thought to have power in the home, and the god of the fields could bring good crops and rain. The temple gods were considered to be more powerful than the gods of the home or the field, and so the images of these gods might be imposing statues skilfully cut from huge stone. Many such idols of different sizes were found some years ago when an expedition went to Asia and discovered the place where the old city of Ur used to be.

Among the nomads, however, there were different ideas of God. We have learned that in those days, each separate tribe believed in a god of its own. The feeling of the tribes for their own God was a very close feeling, like that of a father and his children. Their God would protect them and help them, and they in turn would worship Him and obey Him. On special occasions, they would pick out a fine, perfect young goat or sheep and bring it to an altar to be offered to their God as a sacrifice or burnt-offering. This would be their way of thanking God for His help or His kindness. The names they

had for their God showed how they respected and trusted Him. They called him "The Lofty One," and "The Eternal One," and the "God on High."

The ancient stories of our people tell us that Abraham's idea of God was very much like this. The names of God in Genesis, the first book of the Bible, are like the names we just told about. Abraham thought of only one God who would help him and protect him. This was the God Abraham had chosen for himself and for his tribe. He could not see his God and did not need wooden or clay or even golden images of Him.

Now we come to the reason the Bible gives for Abraham's journey. It tells us that Abraham heard God's voice speaking to him, ordering him to leave Haran and to settle with his tribe in another land which He would give him. With the command was a wonderful promise that in this good land Abraham would become the father of a great nation and of many descendants.

So the caravan of Abraham and his tribe moved on day after day, west and then south, until finally they came to the River Jordan and crossed over into Canaan. This seemed to be the very place they were seeking. Abraham believed it was the land his God had promised him. There the wanderers rested and made plans to settle.

The herdsmen took the flocks out to pasture on the green grass. They set up their tents of woven goats' hair. The women busied themselves with their many tasks. They wove new cloth and made fresh garments for their families. They soaked the skins of goats and sheep and stretched them to make leather for water bags and for sandals and for other useful articles. The men looked for a little plot of ground to grow grain and vegetables. It was good to be settled for a while. Later on they would move to another place to find good pasture again for their animals.

One of the interesting stories in the Bible gives us a good idea of the kind of man Abraham was. Lot, his nephew, lived with him. He too had many sheep and cattle and many herdsmen to care for them. After a while, the shepherds of Abraham and the shepherds of Lot quarreled.

"Your sheep are pasturing on the best land!" they shouted at each other. They pushed each other's flocks around.

Abraham knew he must settle the quarrel. He was the older man. He might have sent Lot away. Would that be acting kindly toward his nephew?

Abraham said, "Don't let us quarrel. There is plenty of land for both of us. Choose whichever land you wish. If you go to the right, I will go to the left. If you go to the left, I will go to the right."

Abraham and Lot ascended a high hill. Before them lay the land. To the east was the valley, well watered by the Jordan River. It was green and fertile. It was a pleasant sight. There was good grass for sheep and goats. Lot chose to go to the east.

Abraham was satisfied. He journeyed south to Mamre where he settled. The land was not so rich and there were dry areas, but there, too, he found room for his people. Lot and Abraham remained good friends. In Mamre, Abraham made friends with his neighbors. He helped them fight their enemies and he would not take any reward for his help. In all his dealings, Abraham was honest and just. The people with whom he lived liked and respected him.

A wonderful event took place while Abraham lived in Mamre. Sarah, his wife, gave birth to a son. They called him Isaac. Abraham and Sarah rejoiced. Above all, Abraham was happy because he believed that now through Isaac he would be not only the leader of a tribe but the father of many descendants who would believe in God.

Isaac was not Abraham's only son. Abraham had more than one wife, as did most of the men at that time. Because Isaac was the son of Sarah, Abraham's first wife, he was chosen to be the head of the tribe. Another important son was named Ishmael. Ishmael became the father of another people, the Ishmaelites. Their descendants are found among the Arabs of today.

When Abraham and Sarah died, they were buried in a cave called the Cave of Machpelah. In the city of Hebron, which is supposed to be on the site of ancient Mamre, there is a cave with this name. It is sacred both to Jews and Arabs. Abraham, the father of two great peoples, is buried there.

The stories in the Bible tell us about Abraham, Isaac, and Jacob. They were the ancestors of a group of people who gradually began to believe in one God who could not be seen. They opposed making and worshipping idols. As the years went by, these men and women developed their own religion, their own ways of living and fine ideas about how to treat their fellow men. From their midst came valiant heroes and leaders who taught the world some of its most important ideas. They were the Jewish people and their story began with Abraham.

A MAP ACTIVITY

Examine the map on page 13. Make an outline map and put in the cities where Abraham lived. Color the Fertile Crescent green. Show the Tigris, Euphrates, and Jordan Rivers. Write the names Arabian Desert, Mesopotamia, Canaan and Egypt in their proper places.

SOMETHING TO TALK OVER IN CLASS

Where do tribes of nomads live today?

Is life for a nomad easier or harder than life for a settled person? What advantages or disadvantages are there in these two ways of living?

SOMETHING TO DO

Make a list of some foods you think a nomad child might have eaten. What foods do you eat that he would not have known about?

READ

The Story of Genesis by Adele Bildersee, pp. 24–29.

How the Early Hebrews Lived and Learned by Edna M. Bonser, pp. 1–15.

A *Picture Dictionary of the Bible* by Ruth P. Tubby is a good book to keep in your room.

A MOVIE TO SEE

Ask your teacher to order "Desert Nomads." It is a good picture of nomads today and will give you an idea of the way nomads lived long ago.

Order from United World Films, 1445 Park Avenue, New York 29, N. Y.

Unit 2

How the Hebrews Became
a Free People

A large caravan of Hebrews went down from Canaan to Egypt to escape a serious famine in the land. From this journey, came a series of events which started the Hebrews on the road to becoming a nation.

The story of the Hebrews in Egypt and their flight from the country which held them in slavery is one of the most dramatic ever told. Its hero was a man who taught the Hebrews a way of life through the worship of God. They passed on his laws and his teachings through the generations to our own day. Again and again in our prayers and blessings, we hear the phrase, "in remembrance of the departure from Egypt."

Let us see what happened to the Hebrews in Egypt and how they won their freedom.

Let My people go!

3. A NEW HOME

IN THE land of Canaan, Abraham's tribe lived a simple life. From the stories of the Bible and from other stories of the time of the Patriarchs, we know that they roamed freely from place to place with their flocks. They would come back from time to time to one town which was their center, where the head of the tribe lived, and where festivals were observed and sacrifices took place.

This is the way Isaac lived too. When it was time for Isaac to marry, Abraham sent all the way back to Haran for a wife for his son. Isaac's cousin, Rebekah, made the long trip across the desert to come to Canaan. It was wise for Isaac to marry someone who would fit in with his family customs, and who could easily be taught about his God.

Isaac's life was quiet and peaceful. His flocks flourished. He dug wells which gave water to his people and his cattle. He reared his sons and took care of his shepherds and their families. He made a treaty with a neighboring king to live peacefully together. When he and Rebekah died, they were buried in the Cave of Machpelah.

Jacob, his son, lived a more adventurous life. You remember the Bible tale which tells how he had to flee from home, away from his brother Esau. He went to Haran, to the home of his uncle, Laban, and worked for him. There he married his two cousins, Leah and Rachel, and had many sons. But he could not stay away from Canaan, his birthplace and home. He had always been told that this land had been promised to his family by the God of Abraham. Many years later he returned with his wives and children and settled in Shechem, which was in the center of Canaan. He made friends with Esau. He lived comfortably in the midst of his large family, and had many possessions.

However, there came a time when Jacob and his sons left Canaan and went down to Egypt. After they lived there for many years, their descendants were forced to become slaves and to work from dawn to dusk for cruel taskmasters.

How did the free Hebrew tribe, whose families had large herds of cattle, homes to live in, and valuable possessions, come to be a people of slaves in a land far away?

The reason is found in one short but terrible word—famine. There was not enough food to go around. Famine brings great hardships—hunger and illness. Famines would come when the rainfall was scanty, or as it happened in some very bad years, when there was no rain at all to water the dry and thirsty earth. This was called a year of drought. More than once we read of drought in the land of Canaan. Grass for cattle did not flourish. The goats did not give milk. Cheese and butter could not be made. Grain for people did not grow. Trees did not bear good fruit. There was not enough to eat. There was famine in the land.

In the large and prosperous land of Egypt, the River Nile watered the earth. Every spring the river overflowed its banks, and when the waters settled, rich, damp soil remained

behind. Food for man and beast grew well. In the picture on this page, you can see the Egyptians selling grain to people from another land. In Canaan, the people heard, "There are good crops in Egypt." Jacob and his sons went to Egypt because of the famine.

Now you must read the thrilling Bible story of Jacob's son, Joseph, and his adventures in Egypt. That will help you to understand how the Hebrews came to Egypt. They settled there with the help of Pharaoh, who invited them to come. He was grateful to Joseph who had kept the Egyptians from starving.

A new life in another land began for the Hebrews. What did they find in Egypt?

Thirty-four hundred years ago, at about the year 1500 B.C.E., Egypt was a civilized land. It had great cities and wide roads, beautiful palaces, and imposing temples. Boats of many kinds sailed up and down the Nile; some were used for pleasure and some carried cargo to and from different cities and countries. The Pharaoh, king of Egypt, was not only the ruler, he was worshipped as a god. There were many other gods that the people worshipped and many priests who took care of the great temples. The rich lived in splendor, although there were many poor farmers and workers and great numbers of slaves.

What a change from the land of Canaan, where the Hebrews lived their simple lives as shepherds! The Pharaoh understood that Jacob and his family would not be happy if they had to live in a city. He set aside a portion of the country called Goshen in the northeastern part of Egypt for them. Goshen was well suited for cattle-raising, and for the little farming which they did. Here Jacob lived with his children and their families.

The time came when Jacob felt his death was near. He called all his children together. He told them never to forget the land of Canaan and the religion which they followed. He said that some day they must return to Canaan and asked them to take him along to bury him in the Cave of Machpelah together with Abraham and Isaac. His children sadly made him this promise.

After many years, Joseph and Benjamin and all the other brothers passed away. Their children remained in Goshen. There they were happy and comfortable. There was food to eat, good land for their cattle; the climate was pleasant. They learned a great deal from their Egyptian neighbors. They must have seen that it was more pleasant to live in houses made of brick than in tents made of goatskin and cloth. The winds would blow through the thin tents. The rains would soon drip on to the mats inside. Even though the bricks might have been made of dried earth and clay, they made a cozy little house, where a family could live very comfortably.

The Egyptians had important skills which raised them high on the scale of civilization. They had the tools for learning that you use today. Stop here a moment to make up your mind what they are. Have you decided? Do you agree that reading and writing are the tools of learning? The Egyptians had a system of writing. At first they used pictures to stand for words. Then they improved their system. They made signs to stand for sounds.

From the Nile River the Egyptians took thick reeds called papyrus. From these reeds they learned to make sheets of something like paper which had a fine, smooth surface on which to write. For pens they had thin reed quills, and their ink was made of soot and oil or thin glue. Only the priests and some of the nobles could read and write. From the "papyrus" of the old Egyptians comes our own word "paper."

The Hebrews did not learn to write while they were in Egypt although some Hebrew letters may have come from the Egyptian picture writing. They did see that there was a new way of remembering people's stories. It was better than just telling them to your children. Later on when they returned to Canaan, they too learned a system of writing. It was similar to the writing of some new neighbors, the Phoenicians.

The Egyptians had other skills and crafts. They had learned about metals, such as copper and tin and bronze. They found out that by mixing copper and tin, they got a harder metal called bronze. With this metal they could make better plows and tools for farming and working. They grew flax and could weave very fine linen for garments as well as heavier woolen cloths. They made beautiful jewelry and ornaments and fine pottery. They used a potter's wheel which made better shaped vessels than those fashioned by hand. The Egyptians had musicians who played flutes and harps and cymbals. Surely some of the Hebrews learned these skills and crafts, too.

Did the Hebrews learn other things from the Egyptians? Did they borrow some of the Egyptian ideas of God?

The Egyptians believed in many gods such as a sun god and a moon god. One was named Amon-Re. He was one of the chief gods. Some of the gods had sisters and wives, and they were worshipped, too. The Pharaoh was also a god, and the people worshipped and obeyed him as god as well as king.

At one time a Pharaoh named Akhnaton tried to destroy the ancient gods of Egypt, and the influence of their priests. He worshipped the sun god, named Aton. But Akhnaton considered himself a god, too, who came between Aton and the people. He erected statues to Aton and also to himself, and built a new city for the worship of his god. While Akhnaton lived the people had to follow his ways, but as soon as he died the priests of the old religion rose and destroyed the statues and temples of Aton. The new city fell into ruins and Aton was forgotten. Any ideas of one god which might have grown out of the worship of Aton perished with Akhnaton.

However, the Hebrews were far removed from the great Pharaoh, Akhnaton. They did not pay attention to his god or to the many gods that the Egyptian priests worshipped. They continued to think of their God as the God of the Patriarchs, who had been chosen for them long ago.

For many years Egypt's Pharaohs and priests and nobles let the Hebrews live peacefully. They remembered the teachings of their fathers. Although a few of them went into the cities to live like Egyptians, most of them remained in Goshen. They lived their own separate lives and followed the customs they had brought from Canaan. There were times when they must have talked about going back to Canaan—but that would be later on. They could not guess that the day would come when they would struggle to leave Egypt and to return to the land of their fathers.

SOMETHING IMPORTANT TO KNOW

Jacob had twelve sons. Their names were:

* Simeon	* Issachar	* Naphtali
Levi	* Dan	Joseph
* Judah	* Gad	* Benjamin
* Zebulun	* Asher	* Reuben

Joseph had two sons. Their names were:
* Ephraim   * Manasseh

Those names marked with a star were the Twelve Tribes. The land of Canaan was divided among them. The Levites were the tribe of priests. They did not settle in any one section of the land.

SOMETHING TO TALK OVER IN CLASS

Why did ancient lands suffer so often from famine?

What do farmers do today in order to grow food in dry areas?

What world organization is helping people who need food by teaching them to raise better crops?

SOMETHING TO DO

After you have read some of the books suggested at the end of this page write a composition on one of these topics:

Ancient alphabets and our alphabet today.

The puzzles of ancient writings.

Some skills of people of long ago.

A MAP ACTIVITY

On your map show Shechem, Goshen, the Nile River.

WORK FOR A COMMITTEE

Pick out an important moment in Joseph's life and work up a little play about it. Here are some suggestions:
The selling of Joseph.
Joseph in prison.
Joseph before Pharaoh.
Joseph tells his brothers who he is.
The meeting of Jacob and Joseph.
Act out your play for the class.

READ

The Story of Genesis by Bildersee, pp. 90–133.
How the Early Hebrews Lived and Learned by Bonser, pp. 147–157.
Lost Worlds by Anne Terry White
"Hieroglyphics and Ghouls," pp. 98–107,
"Working Out a Puzzle," pp. 203–211.
Man and His Records by Franklin Barnes
"How the Alphabet Was Born," pp. 54–63.
Man Is a Weaver by Elizabeth Chesley Baity
"How Egyptians Raised Flax and Made Linen Cloth," pp. 37–54.
Jewels for a Crown by Miriam K. Freund.

READINGS FOR TEACHERS

Unit II (*CHAPTERS 3–6*)

The Bible, Gen. 37, 39–50, 50:22–26; Exod. 1–16:22, 19, 20; Deut. 34.
The Jews, Vol. I, Chap. I, pp. 6–13.
A History of the Jewish People by Margolis and Marx, Chap. II.
Westminster Historical Atlas to the Bible by Wright and Filson, pp. 37–39.
Israel in the Ancient Near East by Orlinsky, Chap. II.

4. OUT OF BONDAGE

ALTHOUGH the Hebrews lived apart from the Egyptians in Goshen, they were not unnoticed by the Pharaoh and his advisers. Changes were taking place in Egypt. The Pharaoh was fighting on many borders of his land. He was beset by enemies. He looked around and saw the men and women who lived in Goshen. They were not Egyptians. They were strangers from Canaan. The advisers of the king talked about them. Many of the nobles were jealous of the Hebrews, for Goshen had rich and fertile soil. Perhaps, they said, the Hebrews might some day rise up against Egypt. They must not be allowed to grow too powerful. The good that Joseph had done for Egypt was forgotten. The promises of the Pharaoh of long ago were set aside. The pleasant years came to an end.

Then began a hard time for the Hebrews. Harsh laws against them were passed. Men and women were taken as slaves to build the great pyramids and temples. An order was given: Every Hebrew baby boy was to be thrown into the Nile River.

Slavery is a cruel word. It is a cruel act to enslave men. To live as slaves was especially difficult for the Hebrews who were used to the free and open life of herdsmen going freely from place to place with their flocks. The Egyptian overseers seemed to take special delight in making the life of the Hebrews as bitter as possible.

Can anything good come from such an evil thing as slavery? Who knows if the Hebrews living comfortably in Egypt would ever have returned to Canaan if it had not been for this bitter slavery? Who knows if they might not gradually have begun to live like Egyptians, think like Egyptians, and in the end worship the gods of the Egyptians?

The Hebrews struggled against their bondage. They looked for a leader to save them. Only a man of extraordinary ability and character could be such a leader. They found this man—Moses.

The name, Moses, stands out like a great shining light in the midst of a dark night. From his childhood his life was different from that of his companions. Though he was born a Hebrew, he was brought up and educated as an Egyptian by

the princess of Egypt. His mother, who became his nurse, told him stories of his ancestors, and of the God of the Hebrews. As he grew up, strong and proud, he seemed to be a young Egyptian noble, but he knew that he was a Hebrew. He remembered his family. He learned to know his brother, Aaron, and his sister, Miriam. He could not bear to see his people in slavery. One day he struck and killed an Egyptian overseer who was beating a Hebrew. After this act, Moses had to flee from Egypt.

Moses' adventures are told in the Bible. He went to the western desert in the land of Midian. He came to the home of Jethro, a priest of Midian. Jethro welcomed him, and in time Moses married Zipporah, Jethro's daughter. He became a shepherd like his ancestor, Abraham. Day after day he went out with his flocks into the great wilderness. Here, under the open sky, he had time to think and to dream.

He thought about his days in the royal court of the Pharaoh, and of the life there. Could the Pharaoh who was a man like himself be a god? Could those great statues which were made by men be gods? In the great Egyptian city, Moses had seen men from other countries offer up sacrifices and worship their gods. Many of these foreign religious customs were unpleasant and ugly. A great deal of Egyptian worship had to do with what would happen after a man died. That is why the Pharaohs and nobles built huge pyramids and filled them with costly furnishings. They believed they would use them after they had died. Untold thousands of slaves worked and died to build the pyramids.

As Moses sat alone watching his flock, his ideas about God became clear to him. The Hebrews could have only one God who could not be seen. Their God would love them and protect them. In return for His help, they had their duties to perform. They were to worship Him alone and make no images of their God. To their fellow men, they must be honest and just and fair. You will see how Moses added to the religious ideas which the Hebrews had received from Abraham, and gave his people a religion of justice and laws of right and wrong. But these teachings had to wait for a better time.

Moses could not forget the Hebrews living in slavery in Egypt. He saw a vision of them leaving the land of bondage, returning a free people to their ancient home in Canaan. How could they go? They needed a leader who could inspire them with courage and daring. Who would take them out of Egypt?

Moses believed that God called to him and gave him that great task. He spoke to Jethro about his longing to help his brethren. Jethro said to him, "Go in peace."

Moses decided to return to Egypt. He met his brother, Aaron, who promised to help him. They gathered together the elders of Israel. These men believed in Moses. Secretly, they met to make plans for the Hebrews to leave Egypt. Moses and Aaron came before the Pharaoh and pleaded with him, "Let my people go."

"No!" thundered the mighty Pharaoh, the king who was worshipped as a god. It seemed to be the end. Moses could do no more. He believed that only God could free the Hebrews.

The Bible tells how one misfortune after another struck Egypt. Locusts, vermin, darkness, even death came upon the land. At last the Pharaoh was convinced that the God of the Hebrews had sent the plagues and that only when they left

Egypt would good fortune come once more to his country. He called Moses to the palace and ordered him to leave at once with all his people.

Quickly the Hebrews gathered their families together. They packed their possessions on donkeys. Hastily they took in their flocks from the fields. There was hardly time to prepare food for the journey. From this part of the Bible story comes the custom of eating matso, for the bread was unleavened and did not have time to rise properly. They did not care about that. The main thing was to leave quickly.

So the Exodus began. Thousands of men, women and children went on the march.

There were many routes open to Moses. One direct way would have brought the Hebrews to Canaan in a short time.

Moses did not choose this route. This would not give him enough time to organize his people and to get to know them. He could not bring a mob of men and women into a new country. They hardly knew what lay ahead of them. There was much to learn. They had to be prepared for their new life. They had to learn how to live as free and independent men.

The Hebrews slowly marched southward, leaving the green and fertile land of Goshen and coming to the wilderness of Ethan. There they came to a narrow crossing near a body of water which in English is called the Red Sea, though it is not the Red Sea of modern times. Its Hebrew name is the "Sea of Reeds." They moved slowly, keeping the stragglers together, and holding back those who would push forward. To the front and at the rear, they had scouts to hold the lines and to see that all was going well.

Only a few days after they left Egypt, the scouts at the rear brought frightening news. Close behind were Pharaoh and his warriors with horses and chariots. They had come to bring the Hebrews back to Egypt and to slavery. It would not be long before they would overtake the marchers.

What could be done? Behind them were Pharaoh's soldiers —in front the waters of the Sea of Reeds.

Before the frightened and bewildered eyes of the Hebrews an astonishing thing happened. A great wind blew up. It parted the waters of the Sea of Reeds. To those who watched, it seemed like a miracle, and that is how it was related again and again to their children and descendants. Timidly at first and then with greater confidence they went forward. They fled across on the sea-bed. Most of them were over when

Pharaoh and his men caught up with them. They, too, began to cross the sea. The Hebrews pushed ahead faster and faster. They reached the banks of the other side safely. But what was happening? There was a sudden shift of the wind and the waters came together. The Egyptians in the midst of the sea were drowned. The Hebrews were saved.

SOMETHING TO TALK OVER IN CLASS

Has slavery been entirely wiped out in the world today? If not, where is it still found? Can we do anything about it? What other people besides the Hebrews have struggled against tyrants to win freedom?

Did Moses' early life as an Egyptian prince help him later? If so, how?

SOMETHING TO DO

Imagine the time when Aaron brought Moses to a secret meeting of the Elders of Israel. Hold such a meeting in your room. Select people for the parts of Moses, Aaron, and the heads of tribes. Talk over the chances of a dash for freedom.

READ

Out of the House of Bondage by Adele Bildersee, pp. 3–47.
Great Jewish Women by Elma E. Levinger
 "Jochebed," p. 27.
Second Bible Legend Book by Lillian S. Freehof
 "Let My People Go," p. 23.

5. THE LAWS OF MOSES

NOW AT last the Hebrews were really free. Never again would the Egyptians try to bring them back to slavery. A new life opened up before them.

It was not an easy beginning. To cross the wilderness could not be a simple matter. The leader of a caravan would plan carefully for weeks before he began such a journey. Moses had taken the Israelites out quickly, without preparation, and many of the people did not know how to act when hard and unexpected things happened to them.

What do you need most on a trip across the desert—water and food. Sometimes there were days when no water was in sight, when the goatskins, which should have been carrying an extra supply of water, were almost empty. Sometimes all the food was gone. Always in the nick of time Moses found food and water.

There were good times too. Once the band of wanderers found a wonderful oasis of many springs and fine palm trees. There they camped for a whole month and refreshed themselves. How pleasant it was there! In the evenings the families would gather around and someone would begin to tell stories of the days of their ancestors, of Abraham and of Joseph.

Once again they moved on, the men and the women, the

children, the donkeys, the sheep, and the cattle. No wonder
they had to go slowly with such a host of people and animals.
They were coming close to the land of Midian where Moses
had lived when he fled from Egypt many years before. Their
leader decided to let the people settle down for a while. They
needed to get the feeling of belonging to each other. They
had to teach their children what they remembered of their
people and their religion. There had not been much time during the hard days in Egypt for the boys and girls to learn the
story of their people.

Moses found a good place to camp. There was plenty of
room for everyone, and there were grass and water for the
herds of sheep and cattle. It was not far from where Moses
had gone out with Jethro's flocks and where he had made his
plans to go back to Egypt. The men set up the tents and

tended the sheep. Some of them may have cleared a little
land and sowed seeds for grain and for vegetables. The
women cooked and sewed and wove new garments for their
families.

There was much to do. In the Bible we read how a council
of elders was organized to help Moses govern the people. The
tribes were gathered together, so each man knew where he
belonged. Judges were appointed to settle quarrels that might
arise. It was a quiet time—a time of preparing for what was
to come.

How could this band of desert wanderers, who just a few
months ago were slaves, know that there in the desert of Sinai
a tremendous event was about to take place? How could they
guess that their leader, Moses, was getting ready to bring
them a message which would never be forgotten by them;
a message that would be remembered forever by the entire
world? How could they imagine that thousands of years
later men and women all over the world would admire and
praise Moses and call him the great teacher and lawgiver?

Yes, in that far-off corner of the world, over 3,000 years
ago, something unusual and significant was happening. The
people were gathered before Mt. Sinai. They had been told
to be washed and clean and to wear fresh garments. Moses
had been gone for days and they were waiting for him to return. They expected to hear an important announcement
when he came back.

From around the mountain came peals of thunder. The
dark heavens broke into flashes of lightning. The people were
frightened. Where was Moses? They trusted him. What did
he want of them?

At last Moses appeared on the hillside. From the mountain his voice was heard speaking in the name of God.

"I am the Lord thy God who brought thee out of the land of Egypt, out of the house of bondage.

"Thou shalt have no other gods before me.

"Thou shalt not take the name of the Lord thy God in vain.

"Remember the Sabbath day to keep it holy.

"Honor thy father and thy mother."

The listening people were struck with awe. They heard the other commandments:

"Thou shalt not murder.

"Thou shalt not commit adultery.

"Thou shalt not steal.

"Thou shalt not bear false witness.

"Thou shalt not covet."

Moses came nearer. In his arms he bore two tablets of stone on which were engraved the laws he had just proclaimed.

"Will you obey these words of God?" he asked.

The elders came forward. They spoke for the people.

"All that the Lord has said we will do," they declared.

This is the stirring story told in the Bible of how the Ten Commandments were first heard in the desert of Sinai by the Hebrews, and how they were accepted as the basis of their religion and their law. Later on they became part of the law of the entire civilized world.

The first two commandments reminded the Hebrews that they had one God who was ready to help them. The other commandments were clear and simple laws for them to follow in order to live happily and in friendship with their fellow men.

This was the goal toward which Moses had been working. His purpose was not only to bring the Hebrews out of the land of bondage. It was not only to find a better home for a group of wanderers. It was also to bring them together and to make of them a people bound together by an idea of God,

and by a set of laws, which made them different from the nations of the world in which they lived. The Hebrews had taken a forward step in the growth of their religion.

Nowadays nearly everyone knows the Ten Commandments and believes in them. But most people who lived three thousand years ago did not stop to think if their actions were good or bad. They did not ask if what they were doing was fair to their neighbors and friends. They did not think that right and wrong were connected with the worship of their gods. Setting up a system of rules to live by was one of the great ideas which Moses gave to the world. The belief that the worship of God meant that men should act justly was what made the religion of the Hebrews different from the religion of the other peoples of that time.

There were times when the Hebrews did not follow the Ten Commandments; but they never forgot them. Their leaders and their prophets reminded the people of them again and again. They showed how these laws could bring peace and happiness to everyone.

SOMETHING TO TALK OVER IN CLASS

What are a few of the qualities a man must have to be a good leader?

Did Moses have these qualities? Did Abraham have them?

Do you know any laws in our country which follow out the Ten Commandments?

Can you see a connection between the Ten Commandments and some things you do at school? For example:

an assembly for the parents;

the honor system at examinations;

a rule for all girls to wear a simple dress at graduation or confirmation;

no school on Saturday or Sunday.

What commandments do these carry out?

Can you think of other school customs which follow the Ten Commandments?

READ

Out of the House of Bondage by Bildersee, pp. 48–65.

Second Bible Legend Book by Freehof

"The Mountain's Reward," p. 57.

The Bar Mitzvah Treasury, ed. by Azriel Eisenberg

"Remember the Sabbath Day," p. 90.

6. IN THE DESERT

IN THE camp in the wilderness of Sinai, Moses, the teacher, worked with his people. He loved them. He wanted them to be happy. He wanted them to be honest. He wanted them to have faith in the one God about whom he had taught them. He told them how to build a special tent called the Tabernacle, or Tent of Meeting. Another name for the Tabernacle was the Ark of the Covenant. Everyone was eager to help. The men brought gifts of gold and silver and jewelry to beautify the Tabernacle. The women spun cloths of goat's hair and fine linen for hangings and decorations.

Moses put the Tablets of the Law on which the Ten Commandments were engraved inside the Tabernacle when it was finished. The people gathered before the Tent of Meeting when sacrifices were offered by Aaron and his sons, who were the priests. There they listened to important announcements.

Moses taught his followers other things. They began to follow their own customs and laws. Now they were a free people. They could observe the rest and joy of the Sabbath. They did not have to labor day after day as in the time of slavery. And when a year had passed by and the springtime came again, they celebrated their deliverance from Egypt.

Once again they baked unleavened bread; once again they sacrificed a lamb. Even then they observed the holiday of Passover, which is still part of the Jewish calendar three thousand years later.

It was time to come to a decision. Should the Hebrews remain in the wilderness of Sinai? Moses felt they must move on. They had a goal. It was to come to the land of Canaan where their ancestors had dwelt.

Once again they went on the march. Now they were stronger and well organized. They came to a place called Kadesh Barnea. This was not far from Canaan. The leaders held a council meeting. Someone said, "Let us send some of our scouts into Canaan. They can see if we can enter."

Twelve men were selected, one from each tribe, to make the perilous journey. Among them were two named Joshua and Caleb. Joshua was Moses' helper and follower. Moses

trusted him. The scouts left. While they were gone, the people remained at Kadesh Barnea. When the spies returned, there was great excitement. They brought back with them fruit from Canaan. The branches of grape vines with heavy clusters of grapes were so large that it took two men to carry them. "The land of Canaan is beautiful and fertile," reported the scouts. "But we are not strong enough to enter. There are cities with huge walls about them. The people look like giants. We will never be able to conquer them."

Only two of the scouts, Joshua and Caleb, spoke differently. They believed that the Hebrews were strong enough to make the attempt. "Let us try! With God's help we will enter safely!"

But the people were afraid. Moses saw then that more time must pass. The older men and women who had been slaves in Egypt did not have the courage to conquer a land. He would have to wait for a new generation of men and women who were born free to brave the perils ahead.

The wandering began again. The years passed. Moses had done all he could for his beloved people. They were beginning to be united, strong. When the Amorites and the people of Bashan opposed them, they fought and conquered. They were no longer a slave people. They were ready to enter the Promised Land.

There was one important question to be decided now. Some of the elders of the tribes of Reuben, Manasseh, and Gad came before Moses.

"We do not wish to cross the Jordan into Canaan," they declared. "Here on this side of the Jordan the land is fertile, the climate is pleasant. We can be happy here with our wives and our children. Give us permission to settle here and build our homes in this good land."

At first Moses thought it was not fair for them to stay behind while their brothers moved across the Jordan into more dangerous territory. But he listened to their arguments. Perhaps that is one reason why Moses was such a good leader and why the people had listened to him for all these years. He did not want to be their master. He wanted to do what was right and best for all.

At last it was decided. Everyone was satisfied. Yes, the tribes of Reuben and Gad and Manasseh could remain on the other side of the Jordan in the land called the kingdom of Jordan today. They would build homes and shelter for their families and their herds. But the men would join with all the other tribes when the time came to cross the Jordan to fight for the land of Canaan.

Moses was very old. The time had come for him to leave his people. He called them together. He reminded them of all God had done for them. He asked them to remember what he had taught them, to follow the Ten Commandments that showed them how to act towards God and towards their fellow men. He gave them a new leader, the young, wise and courageous Joshua.

No one knew when Moses left them that he would not be seen again. Somewhere on a high mountain he stood and gazed across the Jordan River which ran below. He looked at the land of Canaan. His feet would never step on that soil so dear to him. He filled his eyes with the beauty of the hills and valleys. This was the land of his fathers for which he had struggled so long. He bade a lonely farewell to his people

and to their land. At last he had brought them together. "So
Moses the servant of the Lord died there in the land of
Moab," says the Bible, "according to the word of the Lord.
And there has not arisen a prophet since in Israel, like unto
Moses."

When Moses failed to return from the mountains of Moab,
the people understood. They mourned their beloved leader.
They determined to fulfill his hopes. Together with Joshua
they moved ahead to Canaan.

SOME QUESTIONS TO ANSWER
    What holiday is based on the story of the Exodus from Egypt?
    What special book tells the story and customs of this holiday?
    What is the holiday dinner called? Why?

SOMETHING TO DO
    Write a composition showing how we remember the departure
of the Hebrews from Egypt. Be sure to include:
    the preparations for the holiday;
    the foods that are eaten;
    what the different foods stand for;
    the songs of thanks to God.

SOMETHING TO TALK OVER IN CLASS
    What were some things the Hebrews learned during their years
of wandering and living in the desert?

READ
    Out of the House of Bondage by Bildersee, pp. 80–84, 107–111,
157–160.
    Man Is a Weaver by Baity
        "Cloth-Making in Mesopotamia," p. 55.
    Union Prayerbook
    The Kiddush, Vol. I, p. 93.
    After you have read the Kiddush, you can add a line or two to
your composition on how we remember the Exodus. (Keep in
mind how often the Kiddush is recited.)

Unit 3

Early Days in Canaan

The return to Canaan tested the Hebrews. The first test was whether they were strong enough to take over the land and settle on it. Canaan was the land which was promised to them. On its soil they were to develop into one people, held together by ties of kinship. Would they remember their relationship to each other when they were scattered in different areas miles apart? In this land where life was easier than in the desert, would they remain faithful to the laws which Moses had given them? Would they remember that they were the children of Abraham, who worshipped only one invisible God?

These were the tests which faced the tribes as they returned to the land of their fathers.

From wandering to settled home

7. A PREVIEW OF CANAAN

THE TIME had come. The years of preparation were at an end. Joshua was now at the head of a group of determined and warlike desert tribes. Ahead of them lay the Jordan River and the land of Canaan.

To the Hebrews, Canaan had a twofold attraction. First, the stories of their people had told them again and again that this was the land from which their ancestors had come. This was the land which God had promised to them. This was the goal they had been seeking since they and their fathers had left Egypt.

In addition, the land of Canaan was part of the Fertile Crescent. It looked very inviting to men and women who had been wanderers in the desert for many years. Perhaps we should take a little time now to learn something of the country which the Hebrews hoped to enter and settle.

Have you a good imagination? If so, you can join our transport and go along to the land of Canaan. We will try to see it as it appeared to the Hebrews of Joshua's day. Let's be very modern and take an airplane for our trip. We will have a bird's-eye view of the country. As we hover above the land, slowly circling it, we shall see its mountains and valleys, its rivers and lakes, its dry sands and its green fertile areas. We

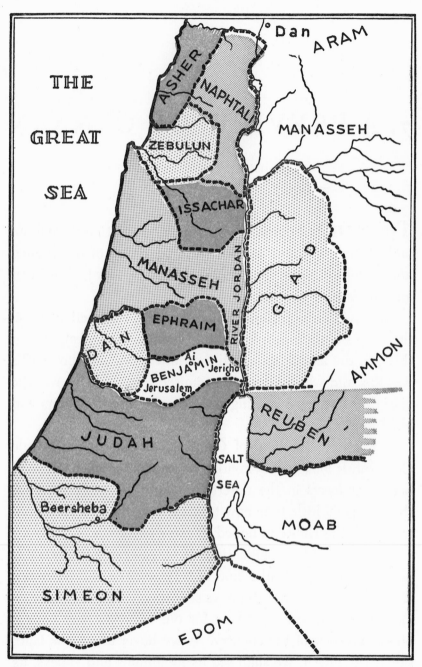

The Settlement in Canaan

shall view tiny villages nestling in farmland, and cities fortified with rocky walls.

Canaan, or as it was known for many years, Palestine, does
not cover a large area. From north to south we shall travel
only about one hundred and fifty miles. From east to west it
is never wider than sixty miles, and in the north there are
places where it is only twenty miles across.

Do the words one hundred and fifty miles mean anything
to you? From New York City to Schenectady is one hundred
and fifty miles. From Chicago to Fort Wayne is one hundred
and forty-eight miles. It is about a third of the distance between San Francisco and Los Angeles, and about half-way
between Jacksonville and Miami Beach. If you live near any
of these cities, you will have an idea of the length of Canaan.

You have probably visited friends who live in a city about
one hundred and fifty miles from your home. It took you three
or four hours to reach there. Your friends did not seem so very
far away. In our airplane we can go from the north to the
south of Canaan in about an hour. If we look down we may
see little groups of dark pin-points. These are the Hebrews.
Traveling on foot with their families and their flocks of goats
and sheep, with donkeys piled high with household goods,
they can cover only a few miles a day. Distances seem much
greater to them than to us. Years later, they will boast of the
great length of their land, all the way from the city of Dan
in the north to Beer-sheba in the south.

We, too, begin our journey in the north, just above Dan,
where the snow-capped Mt. Hermon rises majestically. From
it run small rivulets, and these empty into a tiny lake called
Lake Huleh. These rivulets are the beginning of the most

famous river in history, the Jordan River. We see it like a
silver thread, passing the swamps of Lake Huleh through the
beautiful Sea of Galilee. The Hebrew name for this body of
water is Yam Kinereth, the Harp Sea, and as we gaze on it
from above, its harp-like shape is outlined for us.

As the Jordan River follows its course southward, it falls
lower and lower, and when at last it reaches the Dead Sea, it
is almost 1,300 feet below sea level. Its Hebrew name, Ha-
Yarden, means the river that goes "lower and lower." In our
own day, more than 3,000 years later, the rushing Jordan
River is being harnessed by the new State of Israel, and its
power will bring water to irrigate desert land and to supply
electricity for industry.

But what of the Dead Sea? How did it come to have such a
strange name? In Hebrew it is called the Salt Sea. It is so full
of salt and minerals that no fish or other creatures can live in
it. When the moisture evaporates under the hot sun, valuable
chemicals are left behind. In ancient times the Dead Sea must
have been a disappointing lake to wanderers who longed for
pure, sweet water. Its secret riches were not known. In our
own day, however, engineers and scientists are taking minerals out of the sea of salt for fertilizer and other chemical products. The great Salt Lake of Utah, in the United States, is very
much like the Dead Sea.

From the site of Jericho, near the Dead Sea, it does not take
us long to come up to the hills of Judah. This is the southern
portion of a mountain range which extends from the south to
the north of the land. These hills slope gently down toward
the Mediterranean Sea. Among their rocky crags, goats and
sheep skip nimbly and crop the green grass. Grape vines and

olive trees are skilfully held in places by rocks, one layer higher than another. This kind of planting is called terracing, and is much used on sloping ground. It helps farmers to catch and hold the precious rain which comes only in the rainy season from October to April. In the lowlands, stretching away from the hills toward the Mediterranean Sea, we see patches of green and yellow. This part of the land is good for farming. Dates and almonds, and vegetables like peas and beans, lentils, radishes, and lettuce grow here. Houses cluster together to make small villages. Overlooking these villages on one of the highest hills is Jerusalem. Many of its houses are built of rocks and stone, and the rocks of the Judean hills are used to fortify the city.

Slowly the pilot noses our plane northward, and we come to the central part of the land, to the hills of Samaria. A little farther north we see a very pleasant valley, the Valley of Jezreel. This is one of the most fertile spots in Canaan. It is watered by the River Kishon, and it yields grain, like wheat and barley and corn, as well as fruits and vegetables of all kinds. Lovely Mt. Carmel rises here, overlooking the Mediterranean Sea.

The mountain range continues and we come to the third division, the hills of Galilee. These lie in the northernmost part of the land, between the Mediterranean Sea and the beginnings of the Jordan River.

Now let us cross over the Jordan. Just below the Sea of Galilee, on the east side of the Jordan, is the region called Gilead. This is the territory selected by the tribes of Gad, Manasseh, and Reuben. It is a good place for raising cattle, and has many streams running through it. The most important river is the River Jabbok. We remember that the men of these tribes built shelters for their families and sheepfolds for their flocks before they joined the other tribes in their effort to take Canaan. Further to the south on this side of the Jordan lie the countries of Ammon and Moab, two names you will meet many times in this book.

From above we can see very well why Canaan has been called a land bridge between the great empires of Egypt in the south, and Assyria and Babylonia to the north and east. Along the Mediterranean Sea it offered a natural passage for caravans and for armies to pass over on their way to distant cities. This is a good point to keep in mind. We will see how the geography of Canaan had much to do with its history and the lives of its inhabitants.

Our airplane view of Canaan has taught us many things. We have seen a small country, only about as large as New Hampshire or Vermont. It has great contrasts of climate and soil. We saw the lowest body of water in the whole world, the Dead Sea, near Jericho. There the sun beats down cruelly and the climate is like that of a tropical country. Not many miles away to the east and to the west are mountains where snow falls in the winter months, and where the temperature is cool and pleasant most of the year. Some regions, especially in the south, are wasteland, but there are many fine areas of land where comfortable homes can be built, where farms can flourish, and where cattle can graze and grow sleek and fat.

Now our airplane departs and we leave the land of Canaan. In the twinkling of an eye we are whisked forward in time to our own day.

We are ready again to follow the fortunes of Joshua and the Hebrews of his time. They could not guess that the territory that lay before them would be a land of history and legend, and that its rivers and mountains and cities would become storied and famous.

Instead of the vast dry desert where they had spent many years, where life was hard and food was scanty, the Hebrews saw before them a country said to be "a land flowing with milk and honey." Their hearts beat with courage and hope as they came near.

WORK FOR A COMMITTEE

On a large sheet of wrapping paper, draw a relief map of Canaan. Show the rivers, mountains, lakes and valleys. Write in or draw little pictures showing where:

minerals could be found;
cattle could be raised;
wheat could grow;
olives and grapes could grow.

Show the three divisions of the land—Judah, Samaria, Galilee. Save this map for future use.

A QUESTION TO ANSWER IN CLASS

What features of the land of Canaan would change very little even in 4,000 years?

READ

   A *Picture Book of Palestine* by Ethel L. Smither, pp. 24–31, 34.

EXAMINE

   Behold, the Land by Helen Fine.

   If I Forget Thee by Meyer Levin.

   (Although this is a book on modern Israel, it has many pictures which give you an idea of the land as it was in ancient days. Pick out a few pictures which do this best of all.)

   Israel Today by Essrig and Segal.

SOMETHING TO KNOW

   Lake Huleh was drained by the Jewish National Fund between the years of 1951 and 1958. Today it is a fertile area of 15,000 acres, where cotton, vegetables and grain are grown. A Nature Reserve was set up there, too, where lovely flowers and birds, like pelicans and egrets can be seen. Can you think of other advantages that come from reclaiming swampy land? What disease is wiped out?

READINGS FOR TEACHERS

                    Unit III (*CHAPTERS 7–9*)

   The Bible, Josh. 1, 6:1–6:22, 8–12, 21, 22:1–10; Judg. 4, 5, 11.

   The Jews, Chap. I, pp. 13–23.

   A History of the Jewish People by Margolis and Marx, Chaps. III, IV.

   Westminster Historical Atlas to the Bible by Wright and Filson, pp. 17–20, 39, 40.

   Life of the People in Bible Times by Max Radin. No special chapters are suggested. The book as a whole will be useful for teachers covering this period.

   Israel in the Ancient Near East by Orlinsky, Chap. III.

8. WITH STRENGTH AND COURAGE

JOSHUA'S men were eager and ready. They knew it would not be easy to conquer this country of walled cities and settled villages, well situated in strong positions. The task called for clever plans and brave, almost reckless men. The Book of Joshua, in the Bible, is filled with tales of daring exploits. The author who wrote these stories many years later was proud of Joshua's reputation as a great military leader who led the Hebrews into the Promised Land.

We will see how city after city fell to Joshua and, how in his time, the main conquest of the land was accomplished. That is why we can understand how it happened that Joshua was even given credit for something which may have happened before he lived.

Just as archeology has helped to prove the truth of many Bible stories, it sometimes raises questions on some of the events of the Bible which the archeologists cannot answer. This is the case with one of the most exciting stories about Joshua—the capture of Jericho. According to the Bible, Jericho was the first city in Canaan to fall to Joshua. After seven days of mysterious marching about the city, the walls crum-

bled and fell. Joshua's men entered and completely destroyed the city.

For years scholars, historians, and archeologists have puzzled over the story of Jericho. They read and reread the Biblical account. They sift again the ashes of the ancient city. They have not reached a conclusion. Some say Jericho was in ruins for about one hundred years before the Hebrews entered Canaan. It was either destroyed by an earthquake or by an earlier band of nomads who crossed the Jordan and fell on the city. Parts of ancient Jericho have already been uncovered, and visitors can gaze on great stones which were once houses. Somewhere among them is the secret of the fall of Jericho. These stones of antiquity may some day reveal their story to the world.

But Joshua did achieve many other important victories. His motto was Chazak v'emats, "Be strong and of good courage!" He believed that he had heard God speak to him and say, "Be strong and of good courage for I am with you, as I was with Moses, your teacher." With these words in his heart, he led his men to their first great victory in Canaan, the capture of the city of Bethel.

This was not easy. Joshua had to make two attempts to take the city. At first he sent only a small force of men. Soon the runners came back with bad news. The Hebrews had been defeated. Many fell in battle.

Joshua had to think very carefully. He divided his men into two groups. One group lay in ambush behind Bethel. The other came marching toward the city. The men of Bethel came out to meet the Hebrews in battle. The Hebrews ran away. After them the men of Bethel came running, leaving their city undefended. Then the first group of warriors, watching from ambush, rushed in to take the city. The men of Bethel were caught between the two forces. The city was captured.

The news spread about the countryside. In the villages the people heard of the strength and determination of the newcomers. Some Canaanites did not want to fight. The people of Gibeon, who lived nearby, wanted to be friends with the Hebrews. They were ready to permit the newcomers to settle near their cities and villages. How could they make a treaty with them? The Gibeonites hit upon a plan.

Some of the men of Gibeon were chosen to go to Joshua and ask him to be their friend. They wanted to make him think that they had come from far away. They put on old patched clothes, worn and stained as though they had been traveled in for many days. They carried soiled packs on the backs of their donkeys and moldy bread in their sacks.

"We have come from a far country," they declared. "We
have heard of your victories. We will be your servants. Make
a treaty with us."

Joshua was not sure that they were telling the truth. "How
can we tell that you have come from far away?"

"Look at our clothes and our shoes. Look at our moldy
bread. We have indeed come a long distance."

Joshua and the elders believed them. They ate together and
promised to be friends and to help each other in time of need.
Then the Gibeonites went away.

It did not take very long for Joshua to learn that he had
been deceived. He learned from where the Gibeonites had
come. They were only three days' journey away.

Joshua and some elders went to the Gibeonites. "Why did
you deceive us?" they asked. The Gibeonites replied, "We
did not want to fight you. Let us be friends, we will serve
you." Joshua and the elders kept their word. They did not
make war on the Gibeonites.

But the neighbors of the Gibeonites were angry. They did not want them to be friends with these newcomers. Five kings, the rulers of five cities, banded together. They were from among the Amorites, people who lived in Canaan. They attacked the cities of Gibeon. The Gibeonites called for help. Joshua and his men answered the cry of their friends. Once again the Hebrews were the victors, and the important cities of Lachish, Debir and Hebron in the southern part of the land became theirs.

Other cities came into the possession of the Hebrews in a different way. We think that they entered some villages and made friendly treaties with the inhabitants. It was good to come in and settle peacefully among the people of Canaan.

There were parts of Canaan that did not have to be fought for. The tribes of Ephraim and part of Manasseh settled in the central plain, but there is no record of any fighting to gain this area. It is possible that in this part of the land there were Hebrews already living, families that had never left Canaan to go to Egypt. They would welcome their kinsmen back and share the land with them.

Farther north some of the tribes, Issachar, Zebulun, Naphtali, and Asher were pushing forward. They also met with success. On the plain of Merom they fought with the soldiers of many kings who had banded together. These soldiers had horses and excellent weapons, better than those of the Hebrews. It needed more than weapons to win that day. It needed stout hearts and a feeling of fighting for their own land which had been promised to their forefather, Abraham. It needed all that Joshua had taught his men: to take their enemies by surprise, to make sudden breaks in the ranks and

to strike quickly. They had these qualities and they won the
day.

After these battles the Hebrews could be found in almost
the whole of Canaan. From the north to the south and on
both sides of the Jordan River there were settlements held by
them. It is true they were scattered, and unfriendly Canaanite
cities separated some of them from each other. Wisely, Joshua
did not try to attack certain cities which he felt were too
strong for his men. One of these was Gezer which remained a
Canaanite city, and another was Jerusalem, so high on its
hill that it defied capture until the time of King David. But
he had done well. He had completed the task that Moses had
given over to him. He had safely brought the Hebrews into
the land of Canaan and made it theirs for themselves and their
children. Later on, there would be other battles and other
struggles but one thing was clear. From now on, the land of
Canaan became the land of Israel. We can begin to call its
people Israelites.

In general, each tribe settled on the land it had fought for.
Simeon, Judah, Dan, and Benjamin lived in the southern part
of the country, while Asher, Issachar, Zebulun, and Naphtali
entered the northern section. Ephraim and Manasseh, as we
know, found homes in the central plain.

The tribes of Gad and Reuben and half of Manasseh had
their portions on the other side of the Jordan. They had done
their share to help win Canaan for their brothers. Joshua
praised them for their brave help. Now that the fighting was
over they could go back to their families and build up the
land they had chosen.

Thus, settlement of the land began. The days of wandering

were over. Sometimes, the newcomers moved right into houses which they found in the villages. Other families built homes for themselves. Living in tents became a memory. The Israelites planted crops and harvested grain and produce. Every house had a grain pit, where extra barley and corn were stored. Grapes and olives grew on the terraced hills. These yielded fruit, wine and oil. Wells and cisterns gave a sure supply of water. Cattle grazed on the plains and flocks grew larger. In many ways, life for the Israelites became easier.

What else was needed? What of the teachings of Moses and Abraham? How could these laws be remembered so that the Israelites would live as they had been taught? Where would they give thanks to God for the land He had given them, and for bringing them from slavery into freedom?

A central religious place was chosen, the city of Shiloh. The Ark of the Covenant, the Tent of Meeting, was brought there by Phineas, the priest, and his son, and other men from the tribe of Levi. They were the descendants of Aaron, the brother of Moses. They were the priests. This tribe did not receive any portion of land. It was their duty to go to all the settlements and to teach the people to live according to the laws of Moses. Every tribe set aside some places for the priests and gave them food and homes. When an animal was sacrificed, some of it was set aside for the priests. At festival times, they might receive gifts from the townsmen and villagers. The priests became a very important group in the country.

Before Joshua died he, like Moses, called the people together at a great assembly at Shechem. There he reminded them of all that God had done for them, and called on the

Israelites to live according to the Ten Commandments and to teach them to their children.

Farewell, Joshua! You were strong in war and wise in peace. To this day, we remember the words you lived by, "Chazak v'emats."

SOMETHING TO TALK OVER IN CLASS

In what ways did the life of the Hebrews change after they settled in Canaan?

What made Joshua a good military leader?

Suppose you were a Hebrew child who had lived in the desert all your life. What would you hope for in the land of Canaan?

READ

Into the Promised Land by Jacob D. Schwarz, pp. 11–17 (begin with the second paragraph on page 11).

The Burning Bush by Joseph Gaer
    "Thirty Hours Longer," p. 167.

9. WHEN THE JUDGES JUDGED

AFTER Joshua died, one of the first persons to help the Israelites make Canaan their own was a woman. Her name was Deborah. She was a Judge in Israel.

Deborah was not the first judge. You remember that even in the wilderness Moses appointed some elders to judge the people, to settle quarrels, and to give advice. In Canaan, too, the custom of having judges was followed. But, there was a difference. These judges were chiefly military leaders who united the people in time of trouble.

This time is known as the period of the Judges. It lasted about two hundred years. In general, it covers the years when the Israelites were struggling to keep the places they had won in their early conquests and were trying to strengthen their hold on the land. Often a judge was known as a wise or strong person in his village or among his tribe. When enemies swooped down on the land the judge would be called on to lead the people against their foes. Sometimes after a judge had won a military success, and his name became famous, people would come to consult him on other matters. He would be asked to settle quarrels, and to give advice. That is how the Judges came to be rulers when the fighting was over.

The Israelite settlements dotted the countryside. The first task of the newcomers was to make their homes and villages secure. Then they had to learn to live a settled life. They were no longer wanderers. Some of their Canaanite neighbors were friendly. From them the newcomers learned many ways to live comfortably. They found wells and springs and good places for flocks to pasture. They used the same kind of farming implements as the Canaanites did, and followed their ways of sowing and reaping. Some of the people even did more. They began to copy the way the Canaanites worshipped.

In the cities and villages which the Israelites captured, idols and images had been left in homes and shrines. Often these were not destroyed. While the Israelites still worshipped the God of Abraham and Moses, and on regular occasions went to the shrine at Shiloh, some of them also brought sacrifices to these Canaanite idols. They were told by their Canaanite neighbors that these gods would help them have good weather and good crops. The Commandment which forbade making graven images of God became dim in the minds of these Israelites.

A new difficulty arose. The tribes were not united. Simeon and Judah in the south were separated from Asher and Issachar in the north. Gad and Reuben on the other side of the Jordan had very little to do with Manasseh and Ephraim in the central plain. Each was going its own separate way. Only a great need could bring them together. That is exactly what happened.

Some of the Canaanite clans were very warlike. They

prowled about the roads and fell on travelers. They stole the stored-up grain. Once they banded together under Jabin who was called King of Canaan. They attacked some of the scattered Israelite families in the central plain. The Israelites were brave and strong and ready to fight, but they needed a leader. Who would unite them and bring them victory? Who, but Deborah, the woman judge!

When the elders of the tribes came to her asking for help, Deborah knew what to do. She called for Barak, son of Avinoam, a well-known warrior. When he appeared she ordered, "Go to Mount Tabor, with ten thousand men. The Lord will make you victorious over Sisera, leader of the Canaanites." Barak replied, "Only if you come with me, will I go." With Deborah at his side, Barak gathered men. There was union among the tribes. Fighting men came from Naphtali and Zebulun, from Issachar, from Benjamin, and from Ephraim. They rallied around the battle cry, "To the help of God against the mighty!"

Yes, they were fighting again as Israelites, as followers of Moses and of Joshua. The Canaanite idols meant nothing to them. They were ashamed that they had brought sacrifices to images of clay and wood. Deborah reminded them that they must never forget the God who had led them out of the wilderness and whose law they had accepted when they heard the Ten Commandments.

A great battle was fought near Mount Tabor alongside of the River Kishon. The Canaanites had massed their chariots on the plain. The Israelites were all on foot without chariots or horses. How could they be victorious against such odds?

A storm blew up. Rain fell in torrents. The horses stamped about on the muddy field. The wheels of the chariots could not turn. Fighting man to man, the Israelites forced the Canaanites to flee. It seemed to them that the storm was proof that God was helping them.

With the battle lost, Sisera, the Canaanite commander, ran away. But he did not escape. He was killed by Jael, a Kenite woman. The Kenites were of the same family as Jethro and his daughter, Zipporah, the wife of Moses. They were always friendly to the Hebrews.

The Bible marks this victory by a wonderful poem called the "Song of Deborah." It is one of the oldest writings in the Bible. What makes it so interesting is that scholars believe it was composed by someone who actually saw the battle. The exploits of Deborah and of Barak are described in it. First it tells to what a low state the Israelites had fallen. A traveler was afraid to go through the byways of the land, lest he be set upon by the Canaanites. Then it describes the fighting, the storm, and the victory. The tribes that helped are praised. The

tribes that held back are scorned. From this victory the Israelites learned two things. They could be strong if they banded
together. Their greatest unity came when they returned to
the religion of their fathers.

Other judges came after Deborah in those troubled times.
Peace did not last for long. Roving bands of Midianites would
steal across the Jordan River and plunder the little villages.
Sheep and oxen were stolen; the good harvest disappeared.
Something had to be done.

In the town of Ophrah near Shechem, lived Gideon, of the
tribe of Manasseh. Gideon was not satisfied with what was
happening in the land. His brothers had been killed by a band
of Midianites. He determined to avenge their death. This was
not all that troubled him. He saw that some of the customs of
his own people needed to be changed. Nearby in a grove of
trees was a shrine in which Baal, the Canaanite god, was worshipped. Gideon destroyed the shrine and built another to
worship the God of his fathers. Gideon intended to follow in
the footsteps of Joshua and of Deborah.

He looked around for men to fight with him. Once again
men came from far and near. He chose carefully. He did not
want great numbers, but each man was to be brave and fearless. He selected only three hundred fighters and led them
near the Midianite encampment.

Once again the Bible tells a dramatic tale.

In the middle of the night, Gideon's men rose. Each soldier
had an empty jar and a torch. Quietly they approached the
sleeping enemy. Suddenly the Midianites were roused by the
breaking of the jars and by men running through their camp,
carrying torches and shouting, "For God and for Gideon."

The Midianites were dazed. They could not fight back. Many were killed and the rest fled across the Jordan.

While Gideon lived the neighboring tribes did not trouble the tribes of Israel. He was a wise and fair leader. He added to the land which the Israelites possessed. Shiloh once more became the shrine for the worship of the God of Israel. He kept peace among the tribes. When the men of Ephraim were angry because they had not been called to battle he calmed them with friendly words.

Some of the people wanted Gideon to become king. He refused but he judged the people until he died twenty years later. When the need came again, another judge was found.

Over on the eastern side of the Jordan lay the territory called Gilead. It was good land for cattle and for farming. Here were the tribes of Reuben, Gad, and part of Manasseh. They were the first tribes to find a place they liked and to settle in it. To the west they were safe. There lay the Jordan and their brethren. But from the east they were attacked by enemies.

These were the warlike tribes of the Ammonites. The elders of Gilead looked for a warrior to rid them of their enemies. In their cities they did not seem to have a fighter who would be able to drive out the Ammonites. At last someone said, "Let us ask Jephthah."

Jephthah! Yes, he was the man. Imagine a fierce fighting man who lived in the mountains with a band of men very much like him. They obeyed him. Jephthah did not like the men of the city. They had been unkind to him. His own half-brothers had driven him out of their home. Now they pleaded with him to fight for them.

"You will be our chief if you drive out the Ammonites," the elders promised. Jephthah agreed.

Jephthah was known as a man of valor. He feared no man. In spite of this, he tried to save his people from war. Twice he sent messages to the people of Ammon. He asked them to leave Gilead in peace and to depart to their own land. The

Ammonites refused. Jephthah gathered his men and drove
the Ammonites from the land. Once again Gilead had peace.
The elders kept their word. Jephthah became the ruler. He
too was called a Judge.

In this way, there were many Judges who helped the different tribes in time of trouble. However, a group of neighboring people became very strong. These were the Philistines
who lived on the coastal plain of Canaan, along the Mediterranean Sea. In one of those strange tricks that history plays,
the entire country was later named Palestine, after them. The
Philistines were newcomers in the land. They had come from
across the Mediterranean Sea, and settled mainly in five cities,
Ashdod, Ashkelon, Gaza, Ekron, and Gath. Each city was independent, and had its own king, but they were allies and
would make war together. They attacked the little tribe of
Dan and even the stronger tribe of Judah. In time, the Danites
had to leave the southern part of Canaan where they had first
settled and go north.

No Judge arose who could lead the Israelites against the
strong Philistines. What was the next step?

SOMETHING TO TALK OVER IN CLASS
The Judges had two qualities. They were military leaders; they
were also religious leaders. Can you give examples to prove these
statements?
What kept the Israelites from feeling like a united group?

READ
Into the Promised Land by Schwarz, pp. 18–30.
Great Jewish Women by Levinger
    "Deborah, the Woman Judge," p. 35.
The Burning Bush by Gaer
    "For God and for Gideon," p. 190.

Unit 4

A United People

Temporary union under the Judges had been tried. A strong enemy threatened. A religious leader was now the only link between the tribes scattered from north to south.

A permanent central government under a king was the next step. During the next hundred years the Israelites exchanged the independence of their separate tribes for a royal ruler. From the simple rule of a soldier-king who led his people in battle, the country went into the hands of a king who reigned in splendor in a royal palace.

What took place during these years of change? Would the Israelites be satisfied with this kind of government?

Procession to the Temple

10. THE FIRST KING

A GREAT change was about to take place in the life and government of the Israelites. Up to now they had lived under tribal heads. In times of trouble the Judges gathered them together and ruled after peace had come. It began to be clear that in order to live safely and in peace all the tribes would have to be united in a more definite way.

About two hundred years had passed since the Israelites entered Canaan under Joshua. They were settled on the land. They had good farms and had herds of sheep and cattle. Olives and grapes, dates, figs, and pomegranates were only a few of the products of the good land. The hills were terraced and even the rocky ledges were green and produced food. Modern farmers in our own day use this ancient method on hilly land. Corn and barley and wheat grew in the fertile plains. Towns and villages were growing.

Other changes had taken place. Some men had learned special skills and trades like making pottery, tools, and weapons. These people were the craftsmen or artisans. The farmer would come to a blacksmith to have his simple plow or hoe sharpened or repaired. Tanners worked on the skins of animals and turned them into soft, useful leather. A villager might put up his own house, but in the town a rich man would employ a plasterer, a stone-cutter or even a builder.

Were the Israelites different in any way from their neighbors? Yes, for the most part, they still followed the religion which they had learned from Moses. They still gathered at Shiloh which Joshua had appointed as a religious shrine. Here was the Ark of the Covenant which they had brought from Mt. Sinai. Here the High Priest, Eli, made the sacrifices. The Israelites came at holiday times for the festival offerings. Eli taught the young priests the law and their duties. In some villages, the priests found Israelites who had idols in their homes like their neighbors, the Canaanites, hoping they would bring good crops and good fortune. Then the priests would call upon them to destroy the idols and remain true to their own religion, which taught of only one God and did not permit images to be made of Him.

But the Philistines would not let them live in peace. Again and again they made raids on the villages and stole the cattle and produce. Sometimes they suddenly appeared at the village well when the young girls were filling their pitchers and kidnapped the girls. At last the Philistines encamped on the plain of Aphek, near Mizpah, ready for a decisive battle.

The leaders of the tribes came to Eli in Shiloh. They were desperate. "Let us take the Ark of the Covenant with us into the field of battle. Then we shall surely win." Eli agreed. He, too, wished to see Israel strong on its own soil. The Ark of the Covenant was led out triumphantly. The Israelites were confident of success. But confidence was not enough. The Philistines were stronger. The battle was lost. Thousands of Israelites were killed. The Ark of the Covenant was captured by the Philistines.

Eli, aged and weak, waited anxiously at the roadside for news. A messenger came running from the battle-field. One by one he announced the evil tidings—the battle lost, Eli's two sons killed, the Ark captured. The terrible news was too much for the aged priest. He fell back, dead.

This might have been the end. But Eli, like Moses, had prepared a successor. This was Samuel, the pupil who became greater than his teacher. Samuel had grown up in the house of Eli. He was trained to be a priest. He was also a seer, a wise man who understood what the future would hold for his people. Samuel could look into the hearts of men and judge who would be strong and who would be weak.

Shiloh was destroyed by the Philistines. The priests who had studied and performed their duties there were scattered to different towns and villages. Samuel went back to his father's home in Ramah. People came to him, seeking advice and help. From there he traveled about the country, gathering the Israelites together and speaking to them. He called on them to have courage and faith. It was a period of waiting, of gathering strength.

The Israelites paid heavy tribute to the Philistines. Part of the season's harvest and numbers of sheep went regularly to the Philistines. There would be peace for a while, until the Philistines would come again to steal, to spoil and to kill.

For years Samuel went about the country, teaching and advising. He heard a new cry. "We want a king. Only a king can unite us and help us."

Samuel listened to this cry. He was not sure that it was wise to have a king. He warned the people, "A king may be harsh and cruel. He may tax you heavily. He will take your sons to be soldiers." But the people said again and again, "Give us a king. He will protect us."

Samuel waited. Where could he find in all the land the right man to be king for his people? Samuel kept looking. He wanted to be sure.

One day there appeared before him a young man named Saul. He came to the wise man for help in finding some donkeys which were lost. He must have been a fine-looking youth, for this is how the Bible describes him: Saul was "young and goodly, and there was not among the children of Israel a goodlier person than he; from his shoulders and upward, he was higher than any of the people."

Saul's appearance and bearing struck Samuel. He seemed to be the kind of man the people would gladly follow. Samuel decided to choose Saul to be king of Israel.

Secretly, on that very night, Samuel performed an impor-

tant ceremony. He asked Saul to stand before him. From a
jug, he poured some oil on the young man's head. This was
called anointing him. To this very day, when a monarch is
crowned, the same kind of ceremony is followed by a priest
or minister of the land. The new ruler is anointed just as Saul
was.

Samuel called Saul prince. Then he sent him home. At first
no one knew that Saul had been chosen king, but later on
Samuel gathered the people together at Mizpah and presented Saul to them as their king.

Saul did not mount a throne to rule his people. He still
lived quietly as a farmer at Gibeah. He waited for a test to
prove his leadership.

In the meantime he carried on his duties at his farm, quietly
doing his work. He plowed the land and planted the seed. At
last one day, as he followed the oxen behind the plow, came
the call to lead.

He heard shouts and weeping. Someone told him what had
happened. The Ammonites, ancient foes of Gilead, had fallen
on the town of Jabesh. The men of Jabesh called for help.
Like Jephthah, Saul answered their cry. But he did more than
Jephthah, who fought only with his own men. Saul sent messengers to all the tribes ordering them to come to help him
and their brethren. Now the Israelites had a leader, a king
anointed by Samuel, the priest, whom they respected and
trusted. From all the tribes men came to follow King Saul.

Saul and his men fought bravely and defeated the Ammonites. They fled to their mountain hide-outs. The people
of Jabesh-gilead were saved. They never forgot what they
owed to Saul.

The Philistines heard of Saul's first victory. They were told that the Israelites were about to revolt. They were not afraid. They were ready. They knew the Israelites did not have sharp weapons. In all the territory of Israel there was not a smith to make a spear or a sword. Even to sharpen a tool the farmers had to go to their enemies. This was one of the laws which the Philistines had forced on the Israelites.

More than that, the Israelites did not seem to realize that with King Saul their opportunity had come. Many of the men went home to their tribes after the victory at Jabesh-gilead. Others did not understand that they must obey Saul. However, a dramatic act of courage and strategy paved the way to a great victory. This act was performed by Jonathan, the son of King Saul.

From the heights of Gibeah, where Saul and Jonathan lived, they could look across the deep valley. A garrison of Philistines was encamped there. Jonathan made a daring plan.

Alone, except for his armor bearer, but unafraid, he left Saul's forces. Down the rocky mountainside the two young men clambered and then through the pass at Michmash and once again up the other side of the valley. From crag to crag they climbed, one helping the other, higher and higher, until they reached the heights of the rocky cliffs. The Philistines saw them and started forward. Jonathan and his armor bearer took a firm stand. With rocks and javelins they beat off the Philistines as they approached. The Philistines thought a great army had come. They fled.

Across the valley, the guard at Gibeah saw the fleeing Philistines. He could hardly believe his eyes. He called to Saul. Saul gathered his men and rushed after them. They cleared the valley of all the Philistines who had been gathered there. At last the Philistines were defeated. The new king, Saul and his son, Jonathan, were praised throughout the land.

Saul did not rest after this battle. He remained ever watchful. The Amalekites and the Edomites tried to overrun the country. He kept them out. His men pushed back the Philistines when they tried again to steal over the border. People who lived in villages breathed freely again and went back to their farms and their work. There was hope that a united people would soon live in peace on the land.

SOMETHING TO TALK OVER IN CLASS

Who held the people together while there was neither judge nor king?

How did Saul show that he was ready to be king?

A TOPIC FOR A DEBATE

Resolved, That a judge is better for a country than a king. Choose sides and think of good arguments for your side.

READ

Into the Promised Land by Schwarz, pp. 48–65.
Great Jewish Women by Levinger
   "Hannah, the Mother of Samuel," p. 50.
The Burning Bush by Gaer
   "The Lost Asses," p. 212.

READINGS FOR TEACHERS

Unit IV (*CHAPTERS 10–13*)

The Bible, I Sam. 1, 2:1–22, 3, 4:1–19, 8–11, 16, 17, 31; II Sam. 1:17–2:18, 5:1–5:13; I Kings 5, 6, 9:10–9:28, 11:9–12.

The Book of Psalms by Solomon B. Freehof. Introduction, pp. 3–10; and subsequent pages for commentary on any particular psalm.

The Jews, Chap. I, pp. 23–29.

A History of the Jewish People by Margolis and Marx, Chaps. V–VIII.

Westminster Historical Atlas to the Bible by Wright and Filson
   "The Philistines," pp. 45, 46.
Israel in the Ancient Near East by Orlinsky, Chap. IV.
The Songs We Sing by Harry Coopersmith.
Union Hymnal.
Union Prayerbook, Newly Revised.

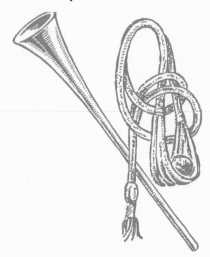

11. THE SHEPHERD BOY

DO NOT think that King Saul dwelt in a great palace with many princes and attendants. In the town of Gibeah where he lived, his home was like those of the townsfolk, a little larger no doubt, with several buildings for his family, his guard, and his advisers. On the battle-field he lived with his men in a tent which was watched by a special guard of soldiers.

Saul tried to hold the people together. To make a kingdom out of what had been a group of tribes was a difficult task. Up to this time, only danger had brought unity. During Saul's reign, the Israelites began to understand that it was wise to be united at all times, not only when an enemy threatened the people. Saul was eager to be a wise and just king. Once he was ready to punish his own son Jonathan with death because he had disobeyed his command. The people would not permit it. They loved Jonathan for his bravery. They saved his life.

In the mornings, Saul would sit outside of his house and people from the different tribes would come to him. They would report on what was happening in the north and in the south. Men and women would come to ask his advice. They felt the king was their friend.

For a while all was well. Many of the soldiers were able to

return to their homes in the little towns and villages. They began to live their usual life again. Farmers worked in the fields and brought their produce to the market-place. There they exchanged it for goods they could not make at home.

But a change came over Saul. The young, enthusiastic leader became ill and unhappy. He had not yet won the loyalty of all the tribes. Some did not send men to help him. He was dissatisfied because he could not rid the country completely of the Philistines.

Saul had other troubles. He had quarreled with Samuel and Samuel was displeased. He believed that he had made a mistake in choosing Saul to be king. He warned Saul that his son would not be king after him. The priest made his own plans. No one knew what they were.

The struggle with the Philistines continued. Again and again they tried to gain back the land they had lost. They assembled a great army in the sight of Saul's headquarters. One day they issued a challenge to King Saul.

"Send one of your warriors to do battle with our giant, the mighty Goliath. Let the battle go to the winner of the fight."

The Israelites looked across the plain. There stood Goliath, huge and frightening. Who would dare to fight him?

At this moment a new figure comes into Jewish history. This figure is so dramatic, so fascinating and above all so beloved, that since his day no one has ever taken his place in the hearts of the Jewish people. This exciting person was David, the shepherd boy who became king.

Samuel decided to find a successor to King Saul. In spite of Jonathan's bravery and fine character, he did not want Saul's son to be king.

As Samuel traveled throughout the land he came to Bethlehem, in Judah, where lived Jesse, a farmer, who had eight stalwart sons. One of these sons was to be Samuel's choice. He saw the seven oldest sons, but he was not ready to select any of them. "Are these all your sons?" asked the aged priest. "There is yet another, a young lad, who watches over the sheep," Jesse answered. "Send for him," Samuel requested. When Samuel saw the young David, shining and tall in his youthful strength, he felt that here was a king for Israel. He anointed him with oil and declared that in time he would become king. Then Samuel left. David once more returned to his sheep. It must have seemed like a dream to the young boy. He wondered if it would ever come true.

The best-known story of David in the Bible is about David and Goliath. One day David went to visit his brothers who were fighting under King Saul. He carried food and provisions which his father had sent. He was too young to fight himself. David arrived just as the Philistines challenged the Israelites to send a fighter against their champion, the giant, Goliath. No one was willing to answer the challenge. The young David felt his courage rise within him. "Let me fight the giant," he begged.

David was led before Saul. How could Saul know that this shepherd lad was to take his place as king? He was struck with his beauty and his daring. He lent him his own kingly armor for protection. David went out to fight, but he soon threw off the heavy battle suit. He was not used to it. All he needed was his sling-shot. His shepherd's training came to his aid. Many a time he had aimed a pebble at the nose of a straying sheep and had brought the animal back to the flock. But

he could use the sling-shot with the force of a gun. Skilfully he hurled a stone at Goliath. It struck the giant on the forehead and he fell down dead. Then David brought back the giant's head to the Israelites.

The Philistines were struck with fear to see their giant leader killed. They fled, and the Israelites pursued them, following up David's success.

At times Saul became downcast and unhappy, even angry. His advisers wanted to help him. Someone remembered the handsome shepherd boy. Saul had liked him and enjoyed the merry tunes he played on his flute and on the harp. Perhaps he could make Saul feel better.

In this way David became part of the king's household. He married Saul's daughter, Michal. He and Jonathan became fast friends. He fought valiantly in battle.

David began to have many followers of his own. His name was known far and wide. A song was sung in his honor. It said:

> Saul hath slain his thousands,
> And David his ten thousands.

Saul became jealous of the young man whom he once had loved. More than once he tried to kill David. At last Jonathan warned his friend to flee.

It was not safe for David to live any more in the land of Israel. He gathered about him a number of men and went across the border to live for a while in Gaza, in the land of the Philistines. Only among Saul's enemies did David feel safe. If Saul had captured him anywhere in Israel, David would have been killed.

Now David was an outlaw, the leader of a band of rough and wild men. They lived in a town called Ziklag which the Philistine king had given David. Though they lived among the Philistines, they did not fight for them. Sometimes they were even able to warn the Israelites and help them.

Once again the Philistines came in great numbers to battle against the Israelites. Under Mt. Gilboa the fight raged. Jonathan and his two brothers were killed and Saul fell on his own sword to die, rather than fall to the Philistines. Saul's reign came to an end in an unhappy moment.

David grieved when he heard of the death of his king and of his friend, Jonathan. He said:

> Thy beauty, O Israel, upon thy high places is slain!
> How are the mighty fallen!

Saul and Jonathan, the lovely and the pleasant
In their lives, even in their death they were
    not divided;
They were swifter than eagles,
They were stronger than lions. . .

How are the mighty fallen,
And the weapons of war perished!

This is only part of the beautiful and famous poem of David's, which is found in the Bible at the beginning of the book called Second Samuel.

Strange to say, at Saul's death, his first triumph was remembered. In the dark of night, the men of Jabesh-gilead, whom Saul had saved in his first great battle, came out and gathered the bodies of their king and his sons and buried them. This was their way of showing honor and gratitude to their king.

SOMETHING TO TALK OVER IN CLASS
    What troubles did Saul have during his reign?
    How did David become well known in the country?
    How did the men of Jabesh-gilead repay Saul's help?

WORK FOR A COMMITTEE
    Prepare a little play about the anointing of David and act it out in class.

READ
    David by Elizabeth Orton Jones.
    The pages in this book are not numbered. Read the first three parts:
        "David the Child";
        "David the Boy";
        "David the Youth."
    Stories of King David by Lillian S. Freehof
        "The Stubborn Oil," pp. 20–27,
        "The Five Pebbles," pp. 37–51.

12. THE KINGDOM GROWS

SAUL was dead. But another had been anointed to be king in Israel. Would David now come to claim his high position?

At first David was accepted as king only by the tribe of Judah. Abner, Saul's general, was fiercely loyal to Saul and his family. He proclaimed Ish-bosheth, Saul's only remaining son, king. Ish-bosheth was not a strong man and he relied chiefly on Abner. Abner was an excellent warrior and served the new king well. He succeeded in freeing many of the small villages from the hands of the Philistines. For almost seven years it seemed that there would be two kingdoms in the land. However, both Abner and Ish-bosheth were killed. From the north and the south came the cry, "Let David be crowned king." Thus it was, and in the year 998 B.C.E. a united kingdom was created.

David knew he must keep all the people loyal to himself and to each other. Only then could there be peace in the land. His first problem was where to live. What city would become the capital? There was still rivalry between the north and the south. It was important to find a place which would make all his subjects happy. The city of Jerusalem, built high on a rocky mountain, was still held by the Jebusites. The Jebusites boasted that their city on the hill could never be taken. Even

Saul did not try to capture Jerusalem, but David found a way. He discovered a tunnel which led through the mountain to the city. He entered Jerusalem with his men and captured it. Jerusalem, the city of Zion, became the capital of his kingdom. It was a master stroke. Everyone was pleased. About two hundred and fifty years had passed from the time of Joshua's entrance into Canaan until David's capture of Jerusalem. Tribal divisions were weakened and real unity began.

David set out to work with energy and ambition. He fought a decisive battle with the Philistines. Never again were they a serious threat to the Israelites. Their power was broken. Then he turned his attention to other people on the borders of Palestine. He overcame the ancient foes of his people, the Ammonites, the Moabites, and the Edomites. To the far north he conquered Aram. As a result of these conquests, he added much territory to his kingdom—far to the east and north beyond the city of Damascus. The conquered peoples paid tribute and wealth poured into the treasury of the king. Above all, the land became safe and secure and peaceful.

Now the new king could turn to other matters. Jerusalem was to be the royal home and the seat of the government. It was also to be a religious center. David decided to bring the Ark of the Covenant to Jerusalem.

Do you remember what happened to the Ark? Where was it all these years since the Israelites had taken it out to battle against the Philistines and it had been captured? The Bible tells how many strange adventures befell the Ark after that fateful day.

At first the Philistines in great jubilation took the Ark to the city of Ashdod. Not long after a plague broke out in Ash-

dod. The people there blamed the plague on the Ark. "The God of Israel is angry," they declared. The Philistines were frightened. They finally sent the Ark back to Israel. After many wanderings, it came to the city of Kiriath-jearim. There it was given over to a priest. He and his sons watched over the Ark. It was almost forgotten, hidden away in a small city.

David remembered the Ark. He sent a party of priests and soldiers to bring the Ark to Jerusalem. At last it arrived. That was a day of rejoicing. The king himself went out to meet the Ark, and sang and danced in the streets with the crowds of people.

From that time on Jerusalem was thought of as Zion, the holy and beloved city. The Ark had belonged to the early days of the Israelites. The names of Moses, Aaron, and Joshua were connected with it. When David brought it to Jerusalem, he strengthened the bonds of his people with their traditions of long ago.

In war there are opportunities for dramatic leadership. In times of peace there is only hard work and many different tasks that have to be followed up day after day. David proved he was a great king in peace as well as in war. He appointed officials of many kinds to help him rule the country. He ordered them to make a census to find out how many people lived in the land. He appointed the priests to take care of religious matters. He began to write letters to rulers of other lands and to have visitors from different countries. He established courts to hear complaints. He tried to rule justly and was himself the judge to whom people could come if they thought they had been wronged. The foundations for a strong kingdom were laid.

On the northeast coast of the Mediterranean Sea lay the kingdom of Phoenicia. The people of this country were seafarers, merchants, and skilled craftsmen. Their friendship and their knowledge were valuable. David became friends with Phoenicia and this friendship lasted for many years during the reigns of many kings who followed him.

Trade with other foreign countries began to flourish. Now that the fighting had ceased, merchants could carry on trade and bargaining. The soldiers could go back to their homes and their farms. Once again the people could use that wonderful metal, iron. Perhaps that does not seem exciting to you, but to the Israelites, iron was a great marvel. Iron came into use during the time of the Judges. At first the secret of smelting iron was closely guarded by those nations which learned it. While the Philistines were in power they would not permit the Israelites to have iron weapons or iron tools for farms and households. Now this was changed. The Israelites learned how to produce iron and began to have this useful metal, too.

David is remembered not only as the brave warrior and successful king. He is also known as the Psalmist, the sweet singer of songs. One of the books of the Bible is called the Book of Psalms. In this book are one hundred and fifty psalms or religious songs and poems. Many of them are said to have been written by David. Some are connected with events in his life and are found in other parts of the Bible. One of them is the fine poem about Saul and Jonathan which you read in the last chapter.

If you will open your Bible and turn to the Book of Psalms, you will find many marked "A Psalm of David." Some of them have an explanation of the time and place they were supposed to have been written. For example, Psalm 18 has an introduction like this: For the Leader. [A Psalm] of David the servant of the Lord, who spoke unto the Lord the words of this song in the day that the Lord delivered him from the hand of all his enemies, and from the hand of Saul; and he said:

I love Thee, O Lord, my strength.
The Lord is my rock, and my fortress, and my deliverer;
My God, my rock, in Him I take refuge; . . .
And I am saved from mine enemies.

The return of the Ark of the Covenant was marked by the
writing of a wonderful psalm. It is number 24, and contains
some lines which must be familiar to you. They are:

> Who shall ascend into the mountain of the Lord?
> And who shall stand in His Holy place?
> He that hath clean hands, and a pure heart;
> Who hath not taken My name in vain,
> And hath not sworn deceitfully.

Many of the great scholars of the Bible believe that a number
of the psalms were actually written by David. Some were
written by other men and at different times. The Bible men-
tions the names of some of the other authors of these beautiful
poems. Because David's reign was a time of victory and of
growth, it was natural for poets to write songs of joy and of
thanksgiving. The psalms seemed more important in the eyes
of their singers and readers when it was said that David had
written them. As the psalms were gradually collected into a
book, David's name, as the author, was attached to the entire
collection. No wonder that King David's fame as the "sweet
singer of Israel" has lasted to this day.

A psalm written by an unknown poet tells what the people
thought of Jerusalem and of their love for David. The poet
wrote:

> I rejoiced when they said unto me:
> "Let us go unto the house of the Lord."
> Our feet are standing
> Within thy gates, O Jerusalem;
> Jerusalem, that are builded
> As a city that is compact together;
> Whither the tribes went up,
>   even the tribes of the Lord, . . .

> To give thanks unto the name of the Lord.
> For there were set thrones for judgment,
> The thrones of the house of David.

This is Psalm 122. This is only the beginning of the psalm. You may want to read it all.

David reigned as king for forty years. When he grew old, his sons quarreled bitterly about who should follow him. One of them led a revolution against his father. However, shortly before his death, David decided who was to be king in his place. He chose one of his youngest sons, Solomon, to rule over the land and people of Israel.

King David died. He left a large kingdom and a people at peace. A wonderful opportunity lay before the new monarch.

SOMETHING TO TALK OVER IN CLASS

How did David unify his people?

What is another name for the city of Jerusalem?

How did David show he was a religious leader as well as a military leader?

Two periods of time are named after metals. They are the Bronze Age and the Iron Age. You have probably talked about these "Ages" in public school. What do we mean by these names?

Where were our ancestors during the Bronze Age? During the Iron Age?

SOMETHING TO DO

Look through *With Singer and Sage*, pages 5–117. In these pages are selections from some of the most famous psalms in the Bible. Select one psalm, or a verse of one of the longer psalms, and memorize it. Recite it at home for your parents.

READ

Stories of King David by Freehof
"The Magic Crown," pp. 140–147.

Man Is a Weaver by Baity
"Phoenician Traders and Dyers," pp. 67–73.

13. THE GLORIOUS YEARS

LONG LIVE King Solomon! Long live King Solomon!" The cry went up through the streets of Jerusalem, as the young ruler, seated on King David's own mule, and led by the prophet, Nathan and by Benaiah, the leader of the king's guard, rode through the streets and pathways of the city. Even Adonijah, his elder brother, who had already declared himself king, bowed to David's decree and accepted Solomon as king.

Solomon became king at a fortunate time in his country's history. He found the country strong. Trade was flourishing. The people were happy to see David's son on the throne. At once he began to carry out new plans. His aim was to bring greater wealth into the country and to make the rulers in surrounding lands know that his kingdom was as splendid as theirs. He intended to rule in majesty and grandeur.

What had been David's dearest wish? It was to build a Temple to God. As a faithful son, Solomon determined to carry out his father's desire. Building the Temple was only the first of his ambitious plans. He began also to erect a beautiful palace for himself and his queens. He sent away to the north to the land of the Phoenicians, to the city of Tyre, for the cedars of Lebanon and for skilled workmen to plan and build these edifices. To pay for the labor and the materials, Solomon sent thousands of bushels of wheat and many gallons of the finest olive oil to Hiram, king of Tyre.

Solomon thought of other ways to make his country grow in wealth and importance. He built roads and encouraged caravans to pass through the land. These caravans paid for the privilege of traveling on the new highways and brought trade and commerce with them. Camels, which desert tribes like the Midianites had used for war, were now beasts of burden for long caravan voyages. Commerce with far-away places increased. At about this time copper mines were discovered in the desert in part of the territory which David had won. They produced great riches for Solomon's court. The king ordered ships to be built by the Phoenicians, and for the first time the kingdom had a navy. The ships sailed away in the king's name to far off India with copper to exchange for gold and precious materials and rare spices.

Solomon had so much gold that he had five hundred shields of pure gold made for his guardsmen to carry on state occasions. How they glittered as the soldiers marched or stood outside the palace when ambassadors from other lands came to King Solomon's court! These men must have carried away stories of wealth and grandeur to their rulers. They might, with envy and perhaps with fear, have described King Solomon's vast array of chariots and horses. He owned over 1,000 chariots and more than 10,000 horses.

After seven and a half years the Temple was finished. Nothing like it had ever been seen in the land of Israel before. The huge cedars of Lebanon, beautifully decorated, made great pillars to support the buildings. The wide courts with their

sacrificial shrines had room for hundreds of people. They must have been dazzled when they first saw the Temple of Solomon.

The king appointed a High Priest and many lesser priests and assistants. These were taken from among the Levites. The new priests were trained in the laws of sacrifice and in the laws of the religion of Israel. Some of them learned to play the lyre and the timbrel and to sing songs of joy and of prayer as they walked in the festival processions. Some priests or Levites were always on guard to protect the Temple.

A great service of dedication was held. The Ark of the Law, after all its wanderings, was placed in an inner chamber called the Holy of Holies. The sacred vessels were taken from the Ark and brought into the Temple. Golden bowls and ornaments were carried in by the priests. King Solomon led the procession of richly clad nobles. Following them came pilgrims from all over the country who had come to offer their prayers and sacrifices at the Temple. The king fell on his knees and prayed to God. He promised that he and his people would be faithful to the ideals and to the religion of their forefathers.

The people were proud of the Temple. From north and south, from across the Jordan, they came to see the Temple, to worship in it and to glory in it. As David became the beloved king, so Jerusalem became the beloved city.

Six years later, Solomon's own palace was finished. Here he lived in sumptuous splendor. The legends about Solomon's wise judgments grew up at this time. The Queen of Sheba came to Jerusalem to see for herself if all the stories she had heard of Solomon's wealth and grandeur and wisdom were true.

A great deal is found in the Bible about King Solomon. In addition to the story of his reign which is written in the First Book of Kings, there are three books which are said to have been written by Solomon. They are: The Book of Proverbs, The Song of Songs, and Koheleth. Although many scholars today do not believe that Solomon really wrote these books, most people continue to think of Solomon as their author. There are so many wise and beautiful sayings in them that Solomon is often called the wisest of all men. You may yourself use some of the proverbs in the Book of Proverbs without knowing that you are quoting from the Bible, and the sayings of Koheleth or Solomon are repeated again and again.

Yes, the stories of his magnificence and splendor were true.

Many of the Bible tales also show how clever he was and how great was his knowledge. He was known far and wide for his wise remarks and for his just decisions. But there is more to Solomon's reign than the picture of a king sitting on a splendid throne, answering petitions. You shall decide if Solomon was truly as wise as legend has told.

While the king was busy building the Temple, the palaces, the navy, and the great highways, some serious events were happening in the country outside of Jerusalem. The people in some of the territory which David had conquered were breaking away. First the Edomites rebelled under a leader named Hadad. Hadad had tried once before in David's time to revolt, but David's general, Joab, had quickly put down the rebellion and Hadad fled to Egypt. Now Hadad saw that

Solomon was busy with many new enterprises. He tried again
and was successful. Then the Moabites managed to tear away.
The greatest loss was the city of Damascus and the nearby
country. This rebellion was led by Rezon, an Aramean, who
also had once fought unsuccessfully against David.

There was one more attempted rebellion which bore fruit
many years later. One of Solomon's captains was a young man
named Jeroboam. Solomon had put him in charge of a division of laborers. He saw that some of the people were discon-
tented under Solomon's rule. He may have thought, "How
would I act if I were king?" One day he met Ahijah, a prophet,
who called to him. Ahijah was wearing a new robe. As he
came near to Jeroboam, he pulled off a piece of the garment,
and tore it into twelve pieces. "This is what God says," declared Ahijah. "Take ten pieces of this cloth. They are ten
tribes of the kingdom of Solomon. They will be yours—you
will be their king!"

Jeroboam's heart leaped. With Ahijah's help he would be
king. But Solomon heard that Jeroboam was planning to rebel
and sent his men to capture him. Jeroboam fled to Egypt. The
king of Egypt was friendly to him and allowed him to remain
there, waiting for a time to strike again.

The kingdom grew weaker in other ways. Do you remember how Samuel, the seer, tried to prevent the people from
choosing a king? He warned them:

> He will take your sons and appoint them to be his
> horsemen; and they shall run before his chariots. He
> will appoint them for captains of thousands and cap-
> tains of fifties; and to plow his ground, and to reap
> his harvest, and to make the instruments of his char-

iots. And he will take your daughters to be per-
fumers, and to be cooks, and to be bakers.

Samuel said more. He prophesied that the king would take
fields and vineyards and a tenth of the produce, and that he
would make servants of the people.

Samuel's words were only too true. Where did all those
gallons of olive oil and those bushels of wheat to pay King
Hiram of Tyre come from? From taxes, of course. Who worked
on all those magnificent buildings? The people, of course.
Solomon divided the land into districts with a governor in
each region. Every three months each man in the different
districts was called on to give one month's labor to the king.

The farmer had to leave his land, the merchant his business,
the shepherd his flocks. To get even more workers, Solomon
took all the foreigners in the land, the Canaanites, the Ammonites, and the Gibeonites, who had lived quietly there under David, and made slaves of them under Israelite super-
visors. He seemed to have forgotten how his own people had
suffered under Egyptian taskmasters. In addition there were
huge taxes to pay for Solomon's great palaces, for his offices,
his soldiers, his servants, his horses, and his charioteers.

The oil and the wheat were not enough to pay King Hiram
for all he did for Solomon. There was still a great debt. To pay

this debt, Solomon gave away twenty Israelite villages to the king of Tyre. They were not large places, but it meant losing some more of David's hard-won territory.

Solomon did one more thing which must be considered when you try to decide how wise he was. His purpose was good. He wanted to strengthen his kingdom. He thought if he married the daughters of kings of other lands he would make many new friends for himself and for his people. Sometimes Solomon's idea was successful. Sometimes it did not work out. For example, when the father of the Egyptian princess whom Solomon had married, died, the new king of Egypt was not friendly to Solomon.

These princesses from other lands were not Israelites. They brought with them their own religion and their idols. Sometimes these idols were even placed in the Temple.

At festival times the pilgrims came from all over the country to the Temple. Jerusalem was the center of the country. The priests sacrificed in the ancient manner. The celebrations were joyful. At these times the people were united and close to their king and their God. But they could not help seeing that even though the nobles of the court sacrificed to the God of the Israelites, they also brought gifts to the idols. Solomon's plan to strengthen the kingdom by marrying foreign princesses had effects he had not dreamed of.

Solomon ruled about forty years. In all these years, his country was at peace. He left a magnificent palace and a beautiful Temple. The Temple and all it stood for would hold the Jews together through years of war, through unguessed hardships and even through exile. Even when the Temple was destroyed it was not forgotten. The glory of Solomon's kingdom might fade away—the memory of the Temple remained.

Nevertheless, Solomon left a dissatisfied people. In the north, there was grumbling against the heavy taxes. Throughout the land there were complaints against the idolatry which was practiced. Even the love the people had for David could not make them forgive Solomon for these conditions for which he was responsible.

King Solomon was dead. Rehoboam, his son, was placed on the throne. Could he command the loyalty of the people?

SOME QUESTIONS TO ANSWER IN CLASS

How did Solomon display his wealth?

How did Solomon get workers to complete his buildings? Would you rather 1) pay taxes to the government, or 2) give a month's work every year? Why?

Which was more important 1) to build Solomon's palace, or 2) to build Solomon's Temple? Why?

A TOPIC FOR A DEBATE

Resolved, That King Solomon left his country stronger at the end of his reign than at the beginning.

SOMETHING TO DO

Get a copy of the Bible. Open to the Book of Proverbs, then to the Song of Songs, then to Ecclesiastes. Read the opening paragraph in each book. Who is called the author? What is another name for Solomon?

READ

Into the Promised Land by Schwarz, pp. 128–163.

World Over Story Book

"King Solomon and the Bee," p. 26.

Stories of King David by Freehof

"House of David," p. 125. (You may wish to read other stories in this book. It is full of legends about King David.)

Down Holiday Lane by Rose W. Golub

"Brotherly Love," p. 162.

Unit 5

A Nation Divided

Dissatisfaction with Solomon's reign came to a head at his death. Heavy taxes, forced labor, and the loss of territory made the people unhappy. The question in the minds of the Israelites was: How would his son rule the land?

The answer to this question broke the union of tribes. They became two nations with different kings. They could never be wholly separated because of their common early history and similar religious faith. The events that took place after the break with Solomon's son show the two nations apart and together.

At this time you are introduced to a group of men who were not kings nor soldiers nor leaders of political parties. Yet they played an important part in the history of both Israel and Judah and left their mark on the history of the world. They are called the Hebrew prophets.

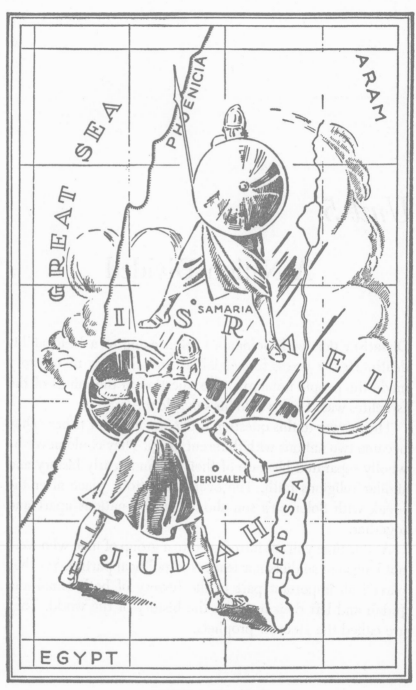

A Nation Divided

14. THREE FATEFUL DAYS

How do you think a young man only sixteen years old would feel when he was crowned king of a great country? All his young life he had lived in luxury. Every wish had been satisfied. He had seen his father tax his subjects heavily. Could he realize that a king should think of his people first and try to make them happy? Only then would they serve him gladly and well.

This young man was Rehoboam, the son of Solomon. He was named king at once when Solomon died. The people in the southern part of the country were loyal to him. He was next in line of the royal family of David. There was no question in their minds that he was to be their ruler. But there were doubts farther north, in the city of Shechem.

Far off in Egypt, Jeroboam waited. At last he heard that Solomon had died. He remembered the strange incident that had happened years before with Ahijah while he was still in the land of Israel. After all these years, it must have seemed like a dream, but he never forgot it. Had the time come to try once more to gain the kingdom? Jeroboam returned to Palestine.

How strong was the union of the tribes which Saul had begun and David had completed? Were the eighty years during which David and Solomon had reigned long enough to weld the tribes into a real nation? The northern tribes had always been a little jealous of Judah because they thought that King David favored his tribe. Solomon's extravagances and heavy taxes added weight to this dissatisfaction. Others in the country were displeased because Solomon had permitted images to be placed in the Temple. Rebellion was in the air. But Rehoboam was Solomon's son and a direct descendant of David. Even the northern tribes would not recklessly break up the monarchy. All the people recognized that the union had brought security and wealth to the country.

A message came to King Rehoboam asking him to meet with the elders of the northern tribes in Shechem. The king could not disregard this request. He came with many of his

court and with his advisers. Some of them were older men who had been his father's friends and officials. Some were his own friends, thoughtless youths like himself.

The elders met with the young monarch. Jeroboam was with them. They asked the king some questions. They wanted to know what kind of a ruler he would be. "Your father put great burdens on us," they declared. "Will you make them lighter?"

Rehoboam asked for three days to consider. His older counselors advised him to promise lower taxes and easier burdens. His young friends had other ideas. Rehoboam foolishly followed his young advisers. "I shall demand even more of you than did my father!" he cried.

Those who heard this answer were disappointed and angry. They shouted, "To your tents, O Israel." It was the signal for rebellion. Jeroboam saw that his opportunity was at hand. He called on the men of Shechem to rally around him. They turned on the king. One of Rehoboam's men was killed. The king fled to Jerusalem to save his life.

Quickly the rebellion spread. Rehoboam found that only the tribes of Benjamin and Judah accepted him as king. Jeroboam was declared king over the other tribes. The kingdom was split. From now on there were two nations, where before there had been one: Judah in the south and Israel in the north.

For many years there was some fighting between the divided parts of the kingdom. Quarrels over borders and boundaries broke out again and again. The rulers of the two countries formed alliances with other strong countries. For example, Rehoboam made a treaty with the king of Aram.

This held Jeroboam in check, for Aram was a threat on his northern border. On the other hand, Jeroboam was friendly with the king of Egypt, where he had lived for many years. The king of Egypt marched on Jerusalem with a great army. He forced Rehoboam to give him many of the Temple treasures and other wealth. The five hundred golden shields which Solomon's guard had worn so proudly went to Egypt, along with other booty. What a blow to the young king's pride; and what a loss to the treasury!

Jeroboam found that something strange was happening. In spite of the division, the people in the northern kingdom were still loyal to the Temple in Jerusalem. At festival times pilgrims continued to go up to Mount Moriah to the Temple which they loved. There once again they would watch the priests sacrifice and hear the songs and chants of the Levites. The Temple was Solomon's real legacy to his son and his people.

Jeroboam made plans to break this loyalty. He built shrines at Dan in the north of Israel and at Bethel further south. He appointed priests to take care of these places and to sacrifice there at festival times. Gradually the people of Israel stopped going to Jerusalem. It was easier for them to go to Dan and Bethel than to travel so far by foot or donkey to Jerusalem. However, Jeroboam did not really understand the love which the Israelites had for their ancient religion. He did something that turned many of his subjects away from him. In each shrine he placed a golden calf. He declared, "This is your God who brought you out of the land of Egypt." For the first time it was the king himself who ordered the priests and the people to serve an image. Many of the people followed in his ways.

Others refused but, because they feared the power of the king, they did not rebel. Quietly they waited for a change to come about.

Side by side, from now on, the two kingdoms were established. Separated, but not completely divided, they went their different ways.

QUESTIONS TO TALK OVER IN CLASS

Can you trace the break-up of the kingdom to events that happened earlier?

In what way did Jeroboam break the religious ties between north and south?

SOMETHING TO DO TOGETHER

Imagine you are having a meeting with Rehoboam and his advisers. Select one pupil to be the young king, three pupils to be his youthful friends, and three more to be his father's advisers. Prepare arguments to present to the king for each side.

READ

With Singer and Sage by Mamie G. Gamoran

"A Monarch's Creed," p. 76. This psalm is said to have been written by King David and tells how a ruler should act.

In the Land of Kings and Prophets by Jacob D. Schwarz, pp. 5-9.

READINGS FOR TEACHERS

Unit V (*CHAPTERS 14-16*)

The Bible, I Kings, Chaps. 12, 13.

The Jews, Chap. I, pp. 29-35.

A History of the Jewish People by Margolis and Marx, Chap. XI.

Preface to Scripture by Solomon B. Freehof, Part Two, Chap. IV, pp. 93-102.

Israel in the Ancient Near East by Orlinsky, Chaps. V, VI.

15. UNDER TWO FLAGS

FOR THE next two hundred years, Jewish history was being made in two places at one time. We shall have to try to remember what happened in Judah while we follow the events in Israel, and also keep in mind how Israel fared when we discuss Judah.

Judah was much smaller than Israel. It had no broad highways to bring trade into the land. Its inhabitants were mainly farmers and shepherds. Its strength could not come from great cities and commerce with other countries. It would never be a great political power. It had to find its strength within itself. And that is exactly what happened.

The little land of Judah had two great possessions. The first was Jerusalem, the city of David. Within it stood the Temple, the religious center of the land, its second possession. Together they united the people in love and loyalty to their kings as well as to their religion, its ceremonies and its laws.

In Judah, the kings continued to be descendants of David, who took over the throne in a peaceful way. When a king died his son became ruler in his place. There were very few exceptions to this rule. Rehoboam's son, who followed him, reigned only two years, but after that came Kings Asa and Jehoshaphat. These two kings lived long and together ruled for over sixty years. Loyalty to the descendants of King David helped and held the people together in bad times, as well as during good days.

In Israel things were different. There was usually rebellion, fighting, and bloodshed as king followed king. In thirty-seven years, Israel had six kings. Three of these rulers were killed by men who wanted to rule in their place. One of these men was king for only seven days! There could be no feeling of unity or loyalty in the country while such events were taking place.

Jeroboam was not able to hand his throne over to his descendants. His son was king for only two years. Then there was a series of revolutions, quarrels and killings, until Omri, an officer in the army, seized the throne. Omri was one of the ablest rulers Israel ever had. He strengthened the country and made friends with the Phoenicians, as David did in his day. He brought Moab back under his dominion and received tribute and taxes from the land.

Years later, the king of Moab finally became strong enough to break away from Israel. He told about it in an inscription on a huge stone. This stone lay buried and hidden in the hills of the old land of Moab for twenty-six hundred years. In 1868, it was discovered. Its ancient writing was finally read by scholars. The king of Moab told how at last he was free from Israel. No longer would he send the wool of thousands of lambs and sheep to that country every year. For a hundred years, beginning with the reign of Omri, the people of Moab had paid this tribute to Israel.

Omri's name was so well known that in other inscriptions which have been found, Israel is called the "land of the House

of Omri." He built a new capital for the country of Israel at Samaria. Sometimes Israel is called Samaria. High on a hill, it was a strongly fortified city, built to withstand attacks from any enemy. Years later when it was besieged, its stout walls held out for almost three years. Omri built up the kingdom of Israel and handed it on to his son, Ahab.

After the early years of separation, Judah and Israel were at peace with one another. Though they lived under different kings, the people felt close to each other. They had ties which went back to ancient times. Their ancestors were the same and the stories of their early beginnings were treasured in both lands.

While Ahab was on the throne of Israel, relations with Judah were very friendly. The kings of the two countries went out to fight together against a common enemy, the king of Aram, or Damascus, just north of Israel. As a real proof of friendship Ahab's daughter, Athaliah, left Israel to marry Prince Jehoram of Judah.

Like Solomon, Ahab was married to a foreign princess. Her name was Jezebel, and she came from the powerful kingdom of Phoenicia. These royal marriages were supposed to strengthen the kingdom. But this marriage had unexpected and unfortunate results.

When Jezebel, princess of Phoenicia, came to Israel, she brought her religion and her priests along with her. More than ever before, priests and idols of Baal were seen in Israel. Jezebel set up the idols in many shrines and protected her priests. While Ahab was fighting to hold the borders of his country, Jezebel was working against the religion of his people within his land. Jezebel believed that the king was an absolute monarch. Whatever he desired should be his. The people did not count. Justice did not matter. Her religion did not teach her to be fair and kind to her subjects. Her aim was to wipe out the ancient Hebrew religion from the land of Israel. The queen was strong, cruel, and determined to have her way. Only an unusual person could take a stand against her.

From the desert area of Gilead, across the Jordan, such a person suddenly appeared. His name was Elijah, and he was known as the prophet, the man of God.

Now Jewish history becomes different than ever before. There are still two kingdoms; there are still kings and princes

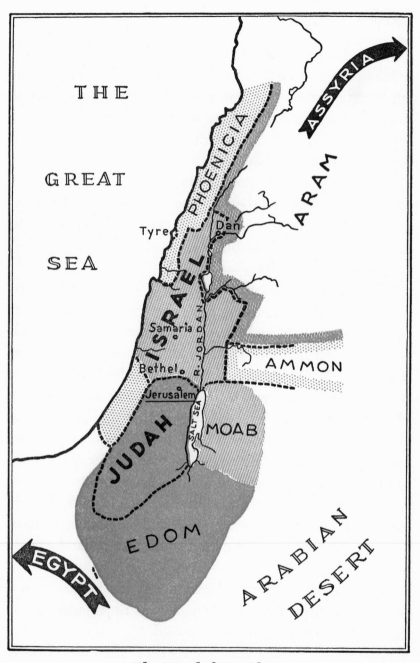

The Divided Kingdom

who rule and make war and make peace. There are still priests who lead the people in worship and in sacrifice. But a new group steps into the picture. They are the prophets, with a message for the kings, the priests, and the people. Before we go further, we must learn who were the prophets and how they delivered their message.

QUESTIONS TO TALK OVER IN CLASS

How did Omri show his power over the kingdom of Moab?

By what other names was the kingdom of Israel known in Omri's time?

How did Israel and Judah show their friendship for each other?

A MAP ACTIVITY

On your class map show the division of the country. Put in the cities of Jerusalem, Dan, Bethel, and Samaria.

Show also Aram, Egypt, Phoenicia, and Moab.

16. THE MEN WHO SHOWED THE WAY

IF YOU go to the dictionary and look up the word prophet, this is what you will find: "Prophet"—one who speaks for God—one who explains what God wishes man to do.

We think of Moses as the first and greatest of all the prophets. He spoke the word of God back in the days of Sinai. From the time of Saul on we hear again of prophets. These men stood out from among the people. Their lives were filled with a great effort—to bring the word of God to their fellow men. One and all they believed that they had a message which God had commanded them to deliver to their people.

One of the prophets named Amos tried to explain this feeling. He said:

> The Lord God hath spoken,
> Who can but prophesy?

A prophet could not help himself. When he heard the message of God in his heart, he had to speak.

The prophets can be divided into three groups. These are the Early Prophets, the Schools of Prophets, and the Later or Literary Prophets.

You know some of the early prophets and what they did. They were not content just to speak. They acted firmly, sometimes defying kings, nobles, and priests.

A good example of the early prophets was Samuel, the priest. He was also called the seer or prophet. Samuel held the tribes together when they were under the heel of the Philistines. He gave them courage by telling them that God would help them. He gave them their leaders when he anointed Saul and then David as their king. Ahijah was another early prophet who acted when the people were suffering under Solomon's rule. He came to Jeroboam and urged him to rebel. He said that God would divide the kingdom and give Jeroboam ten tribes to rule over. Soon you will read of Elijah and Elisha and what they did in Ahab's reign.

The early prophets were men of force and action who fought against those who tried to weaken their people's religion. Their purpose was to keep the people loyal to the religion of their fathers. This meant that idol-worship had to be wiped out of the land. Justice and honesty had to be the law of the land, observed by all—king and common man alike.

The Bible tells about the early prophets. Their messages were not written down when they were spoken. What they said and did was so striking that it was remembered by those who heard and saw them. When the history of their times was recorded, their stories became part of the tale.

The second group of prophets, the schools or bands of prophets, are not so well known. You may never have heard of them. These men usually lived together and roamed the countryside in groups, speaking to the people. When a man joined one of these bands, he learned what to do. Just as a priest was

taught the art of priesthood, so these prophets were taught
their craft. Before they spoke, they might dance, sing or cry
aloud. They might try to foretell the future. Sometimes they
performed astonishing deeds which seemed like miracles to
those who watched. Such actions made those who watched
listen carefully to what the prophets said.

There is a good description of such a band of prophets in
the story about Saul. After Samuel had anointed Saul, he said
to the young man, "It shall come to pass, when thou comest to
the city, that thou shalt meet a band of prophets coming down
from the altar with a psaltery, and a timbrel, and a pipe, and
a harp, before them; and they will be prophesying. And the
spirit of the Lord will come mightily upon thee, and thou
shalt prophesy with them."

Saul did meet the prophets, and when he saw them he joined them, and sang and danced with them. This surprised the onlookers very much, for he was not a member of the band of prophets, and they asked, "Is Saul also among the prophets?"

The bands of prophets acted in these striking ways in order to emphasize one point. They opposed the new religions that came into Israel and Judah, and urged the people to break away from the worship of idols and of Baal.

Jezebel, the queen, hated the prophets. Once she gave an order that all the bands of prophets should be destroyed. Their lives were in danger. Fortunately, this order was never carried out. One of King Ahab's officers hid one hundred and fifty of them in a cave. There they lived for many years.

About a hundred years later, there appeared the first of the third group of prophets, who are called the later or the literary prophets. They are different from the first two divisions that we have described. The first difference is simple. The words of the later prophets were written down at once, or soon after they were spoken. In time their messages became part of the Bible, each in a separate book. There are fifteen books of prophecy in the Bible.

The later prophets never danced or shouted or tried to work miracles like the bands of prophets or early prophets might have done. They tried to make their messages so strong and so true that those who listened would believe that they were hearing the word of God.

These were the ideas which the prophets tried to bring to the people. First, that God wished all men to be kind and just to one another. The rich were told to act righteously and not to take advantage of the poor. They taught that religion was bound up with how men behaved and was not just a matter of sacrifice and worship. Religion should teach men to be kind to each other and to help the widow, the orphan, and any other unfortunate human being.

The prophets raised their voices on behalf of the poor and oppressed. Do not think that Israel and Judah were the only countries where some men were rich and others lived in poverty. In lands like Assyria and Egypt, the poor suffered bitterly at the hands of their rich masters. But the records of the ancient world do not tell of other men who pleaded the cause of the poor man. The words of the prophets stand alone, unmatched.

The prophets declared also that when the Israelites and Judeans held on to their own faith, their country would be strengthened. These men were keen observers and looked beyond the borders of their own land. They watched closely the countries which surrounded Israel and Judah. What happened in other lands was important to their own people. They saw how necessary it was for the people to be united and loyal to the religion of their fathers, if they were to guard and protect their country.

The most valuable lesson was still to come. From the earliest days of their history, the Hebrews had only one God whom they worshipped at first as the God of their tribe, and later on, as the God of their nation. They saw that other peoples believed in other gods. Like everyone else at that time, they accepted the idea that each people or nation had its own god. How did the men of Israel and Judah come at last to believe that there was only one God who was the Lord of the entire universe? It was through the work of these later prophets who developed the idea of a universal God, Father of all mankind. They followed in the footsteps of earlier teachers of their people like Moses and Elijah. As they spoke, over many years, they gradually influenced their countrymen to cast aside the idea of a tribal or national god. It was not an easy task they set themselves to do, but at last the prophets gave to the Israelites and their fellow Judeans the wonderful message of one God for all people and all nations. Through them it was given to the entire world.

Not only did the prophets have these grand thoughts, but they spoke and wrote them in beautiful poetic form. Their lofty thoughts are written in inspiring language. To this very day, writers and speakers quote from the prophets, in speeches, in articles and in books, because they cannot express certain thoughts in any better way.

In a way, the later prophets can be called men of ideas, while the early prophets were men of action. The early prophets worked within the borders of their own country and its people, but the words of the later prophets included the whole of mankind, though they spoke in Israel and Judah. Both groups were religious leaders and patriots who loved their people, their country and its traditions, and who never hesitated to speak out or to act courageously when the time for action came.

In a tiny corner of the world, about twenty-five hundred years ago, these men lived and taught. Kings and warriors of that time fought and struggled. Many of them have long been forgotten. The words and deeds of the prophets made a lasting impression. After all these years, what the prophets said

is still a guide for men to follow. Because of their words, as
you will see when we come to read about them, the history
of the two small, ancient kingdoms of Israel and Judah became an important part of world history. What they said
helped to make the kind of world we live in today, and influenced the life of people all over the globe.

SOME QUESTIONS TO TALK OVER IN CLASS

What are some of the differences between the early and the
later prophets?

What are two important teachings of the later prophets?

SOMETHING TO DO

Think of three or four problems which our country faces today.
List them. Write ten lines on one of these subjects as you would
imagine a prophet might write about them.

READ

The Lore of the Old Testament by Joseph Gaer
    "Jezebel and the Prophets," p. 254,
    "The Miracle of the Pitcher," p. 255.

Unit 6

The Kingdom of Israel

The kingdoms of Judah and Israel were caught in a struggle for power of the larger nations which surrounded them. Israel was torn from within and attacked by forces outside. It showed the world a surface of power and wealth, while its people were sharply divided into groups of rich and poor. The men who spoke in God's name called her leaders to account.

Israel was lost as a political unit. Its people were scattered to foreign lands. It left a great inheritance to the world—the words and ideas of its prophets. They have never been forgotten.

The little land of Judah was left to carry on the religion and laws of its forefathers.

Justice shall rule!

17. TROUBLED TIMES

You HAVE probably read many stories about Elijah, the prophet. In some stories he is described as an old man with a kind face and a long white beard going around doing good deeds and helping poor people. In other legends he takes on other forms. Sometimes he is a young man; often he is even invisible. Our legends say that on Passover, Elijah visits every Jewish home during the Seder. At the proper moment we open the door and the unseen Elijah is welcomed to bless the family and guests.

However, King Ahab was not happy to see Elijah. The prophet looked very different from the other men of Israel. Elijah had lived alone for a long time. His hair was long and shaggy. All he wore was a hairy robe, held together by a belt. He had a solemn message for the king: "Because you have allowed idols and the worship of Baal to come into the land of Israel, no rain shall fall for three years." This was one of the worst calamities that could befall the kingdom. After this prophecy, Elijah fled from Israel, and indeed there was a long drought in the land. There were no crops. Cattle perished. The people suffered. At last Elijah appeared again in Israel and the drought was broken by a heavy rainfall.

Elijah was a champion of justice. He faced Ahab at another time, when the king and the queen had together committed a great wrong against one of their subjects.

Near the king's palace lay a pleasant vineyard. For many years its gnarled vines had twisted their way along the ground and had given their harvest of rich grapes to its owner. King Ahab saw the vineyard. He wanted it. It would make a pleasant garden for him and the queen.

The vineyard was owned by a man named Naboth. Naboth loved his vineyard. He was proud of it because it had belonged to his family for many generations. He knew he was carrying out an ancient custom of his people by holding on to his family's land and passing it on to his sons.

Ahab said to Naboth, "Sell me your vineyard, or let me exchange it for another piece of land."

Naboth was surprised. Surely, the king knew that a man did not care to part with his family's inheritance. He refused to sell or exchange the land.

Ahab returned to his palace and shut himself in his room. He would not eat or drink. When the queen heard this, she demanded to know the reason why. Ahab told her of Naboth and his vineyard. Jezebel was amazed. She believed the king should have everything he desired.

"Do you not govern the kingdom of Israel?" she asked. "Who dares to refuse your request? Arise and eat and be merry. I will give you the vineyard of Naboth."

Ahab asked no questions. Jezebel set in motion a wicked scheme. Naboth was accused of cursing God and the king. False witnesses spoke against him. He was sentenced and stoned to death. Jezebel said to Ahab, "Go and take the vineyard of Naboth, for he is dead."

On the very next day, Ahab went down to Jezreel to visit his vineyard. His joy in his new possession did not last long. As he walked in the vineyard he heard a noise. He turned around to see Elijah standing before him. Ahab knew at once why Elijah had come.

Elijah spoke boldly. "I have found you, O King, and I will speak the word of God to you. You have murdered Naboth and taken his land! You and Jezebel will be punished. Your children will not inherit your kingdom—your family will disappear."

The wrong which Naboth had suffered did not go unmarked. The prophet would not permit even the king to be unjust and wicked.

Jezebel angrily threatened the prophet. He had to flee to the desert again. But he found someone to take his place. His pupil and follower was Elisha. The names of Elijah and Elisha are linked together in legend and in history.

Elisha was a strong young farmer plowing in the fields when Elijah appeared before him. He had twelve oxen yoked together. It must have been far from his thoughts to join the prophet and his followers. As Elijah approached, the prophet

took off his mantle and threw it over the young man. Elisha understood—he was to follow Elijah. He left his farm and his work and went to live with Elijah. He became his servant while Elijah taught him and prepared him for his work.

There is a thrilling tale taken from the Bible which describes how Elijah left the earth. He and Elisha were standing together on the banks of the Jordan River. Suddenly a chariot and horses of fire appeared in the heavens. Elijah was swept up into the chariot and disappeared. Only his cloak remained behind for Elisha to pick up and wear. All those who saw Elisha wearing the cloak understood that Elisha was taking Elijah's place.

You know now that Elijah and his pupil Elisha belong to the group of early prophets. These two are the most striking of them all, acting vigorously to gain their ends.

After Elijah disappeared, Elisha took an important task upon himself. He joined with a band of prophets who crossed the land from village to village, speaking to the people. It was hard to work against the influence of the queen and her followers, but there must have been many who listened gladly to Elisha and his company of prophets. Elisha tried to unite the people under their ancient religion and to free the land from the influence of foreign ideas and rulers.

King Ahab ruled twenty-three years. His sons followed him on the throne, but not for long. Then bloodshed and revolution once more came to Israel. Elijah's prophecy came true. Ahab's entire family was wiped out by Jehu, an ambitious captain in the army, who became king. Jezebel, too, met her death at Jehu's hands.

The new king, Jehu, forbade the worship of Baal in the

country. The priests of Baal were killed or driven out of the land. For the first time since Israel was established, idol-worship was forbidden in the land. This was due in great measure to the work of Elisha and his bands of prophets.

However, Jehu was not a successful monarch. He began his reign with cruelty and much bloodshed. He put to death everyone who was connected with the family of Ahab. This made enemies for him within and outside the borders of his land. Jezebel's father, the king of Phoenicia, was no longer friendly to Israel. Ahab's friends also opposed the new king. Jehu had other troubles. From the north, he was threatened by the kings of Assyria and of Aram, and was forced to pay tribute to both of these countries. Jehu learned that violence did not bring peace and security to a country.

Aram continued to trouble Israel. Once a great army came down from Damascus and besieged Samaria, the capital of Israel. No food could come into the city. The people strug-gled against famine and terror. Just when it seemed that Israel could hold out no longer, the Arameans suddenly gave up the siege and left. Their departure was strange and unexpected, and has never been explained. But they left behind food, horses, and other valuable possessions which Israel could well use. Even Judah suffered through Jehu. The armies which swept through Israel from the north went on to Judah. To save his country, the king was forced to pay tribute to Aram.

Jehu's cruelty brought unhappiness and bloodshed to Judah in another way. His men fell on the king of Judah who was away from home and wounded him. He soon died. This started a chain of events that began badly, but fortunately, had a happy ending.

In Jerusalem Athaliah, the daughter of Ahab and Jezebel who had married the king of Judah, still lived. Queen Athaliah was a true daughter of the cruel Jezebel. When she heard that the king was dead she seized the throne of Judah. She put to death all those who were in line to be king, even her own grandchildren. For six years she reigned, unopposed. But hidden away was young Joash, Athaliah's youngest grandchild, the only descendant of King David still alive. He was a year-old baby when Athaliah came to the throne. The story of Joash is one of those true stories that are stranger than fiction. Away from the eyes of the wicked queen, he dwelt quietly in the home of the priest, Jehoiada. Only a few trusted people knew that there was a true heir to the throne in the country.

Jehoiada and his followers waited until they were strong enough to crush Athaliah. After six years, they brought Joash to the Temple and opened wide the doors. They assembled the people in the courtyards and proclaimed Joash ruler of Judah. Many of the nobles joined in the revolt. The people rallied to the boy king with rejoicing and song.

Joash reigned for many years. He did not forget the training which his kind protector, Jehoiada, had given him. He rebuilt the Temple, threw out the idols, and restored the priests to their proper places. Judah, like Israel, was now ruled by a man who opposed the worship of Baal which had brought so much trouble to the two countries.

During the years which followed, when Joash's son was on the throne, Judah passed through good and bad periods. Then there came a change for the better. For forty years, from 780 to 740 B.C.E., Judah was ruled by King Uzziah, a strong and capable man. He took over his task with a will. He built up Jerusalem and made it strong, and fortified other cities. He encouraged his people in their work of farming and cattle-raising. Though Judah remained a small country, it flourished under his quiet rule, and the years of peace continued when his son, Jotham, became king.

At almost the same time that Judah's fortunes improved under King Uzziah, Israel, too, came under the rule of a strong and able monarch. This was King Jeroboam II who ruled from 783 to 745 B.C.E. Jeroboam was the great-grandson of Jehu, which means that the throne of Israel had been handed down peacefully from father to son three times in succession.

A new era in Israel's history began in the brilliant years of Jeroboam's reign.

QUESTIONS TO TALK OVER IN CLASS

How were the fortunes of Israel and Judah connected with each other?

Who is the best known of the early prophets? How is he remembered every year? Could you prove this sentence: "Elijah was a fearless fighter for justice"?

Suppose a president of the United States died and the vice-president took over the office of president. Then someone said, "He is wearing the cloak of Elijah." Could you explain this sentence?

READ

    The Unconquered by Joseph Gaer
      "Ben Ari Goes Traveling," p. 59,
      "A Gift Horse," p. 125.
    In the Land of Kings and Prophets by Schwarz, pp. 15–19, 27–33, 62–66, 79–84, 96–99.

READINGS FOR TEACHERS

Unit VI (CHAPTERS 17–19)

The Bible, I Kings 18, 21; Amos; Hosea.
The Jews, Chap. I, pp. 35–41.
A History of the Jewish People by Margolis and Marx, Chaps. XII, XIV, XVI, XVII.
    Preface to Scripture by Freehof, Part Two, Chap. VI, pp. 144–152, 158–161.

18. THE WARNING

JEROBOAM II was a vigorous person with many ideas of how to make his country important among the nations of his time. He strengthened and enlarged the kingdom of Israel. His armies regained Damascus to the north and Moab to the east. The roads were opened to commerce. Caravans passed from north to south. They brought goods and wealth and traders into the land. The principal cities, Samaria and Bethel, grew larger. Craftsmen of all kinds improved in their work. In the towns on market days, they would sit at their stalls and display their wares. Pottery, jewelry, fine woven cloths dyed in many colors, shoes, even armor plate for the soldiers were on sale. Farmers came to the market with their grain and their olive oil. Shepherds brought the wool sheared from lambs and goats. It seemed as though the prosperous days of King Solomon had come back and had been transferred to Israel.

This cheerful picture, however, had another side. The wealth in the land was in the hands of only a small part of the people. The city traders were doing fine business with the caravans which passed through the country from Egypt, Phoenicia, and Aram. Rich farmers, owners of great estates, had much produce to sell. Owners of large herds of sheep and cattle grew wealthy. But small farmers and land owners were having difficulties. Years of drought left them without crops. They suffered in other years from the terrible plague of locusts which are often mentioned in the Bible. The jaws of these grasshoppers, who came in vast swarms like an army, could quickly devour the good growth of an entire season. The well-to-do farmers had grain stored away for such emergencies and vats of olive oil held over from earlier good seasons. The poor farmer used up all he harvested each year. A man who owned many sheep and cattle could always save some in bad years. The family that had only a few might lose them all. After such misfortunes, poor countrymen had to borrow money and if they could not pay it back on time, they lost their farms, their homes, their tools, and sometimes their clothes. They moved to the city, seeking work. There were times when they had to give up their own freedom or sell their children to pay their debts by labor instead of money.

As the merchants, the rich farmers, the judges, and the public officials grew rich, they grew even more greedy. They lived in fine homes and wore beautiful clothes and jewelry. They paid no attention to the poor of the city and the country who found it harder and harder to feed and clothe themselves and their families.

In Bethel where the central shrine of Israel was set up the people would come to worship and sacrifice. The wealthy nobles would pay the priests well for special sacrifices. Most of them believed that it did not matter if a man was unjust or unfair to his fellow men. They thought that as long as he brought a sacrifice to the altar, his ill-deeds would be forgiven. Even the priests seemed to believe this and gave honor to those who paid well.

One morning in the reign of King Jeroboam II, the usual crowds of worshippers were gathered around the altar in Bethel. The priests were at their appointed places. Young lambs and sheep bleated softly as their owners waited their turn to make a sacrifice. Everyone who wished for God's favor brought an offering. Each was sure the sacrifice would bring a reward—good fortune to the merchant, good crops to the farmers, and good husbands for the young girls in the families.

Suddenly, above the busy hum of voices and people, a strong voice was heard, speaking strange and harsh words.

"Hear these words which I take for a lamentation over Israel.

> "The daughter of Israel is fallen,
> She shall rise no more;
> She is cast down upon her land,
> There is none to raise her up."

It was as though a chill wind had begun to blow on a balmy day. Everyone turned to the tall, gaunt stranger, whose burning eyes held every bystander.

One by one he called out the names of the nations surrounding Israel: Moab, Egypt, even Judah. In all of them, men were unjust, unfair, evil. The listeners nodded their heads. Yes, that was true. Those were cruel foreign nations. Then there came a change. Now he was talking about Israel, and of her unrighteous inhabitants who crushed the poor, who "sold the needy for a pair of shoes."

This was God's message, he declared:

> I hate, I despise your feasts,
> And I will take no delight in your solemn
>   assemblies.
> Yea, though ye offer Me burnt-offerings
>   and your meal-offerings,
> I will not accept them;
> Neither will I regard the peace-offerings
>   of your fat beasts. . . .
> But let justice well up as waters,
> And righteousness as a mighty stream.

Righteousness, justice, each man dealing fairly with his neighbor, that was what God wished from His people, said the stranger.

Shouts and crying broke the sudden silence. "Who is this fellow who disturbs the peace? Why lament over Israel? Israel is stronger than ever before."

"Go back to Judah and prophesy there," cried Amaziah, the priest. He sent a message to the king telling about the man who dared to predict trouble for his land.

This man was Amos, the first of those great prophets whose words were written down and gathered together to become a book of the Bible.

What a strange figure he was among the well-dressed merchants and farmers at Bethel! He came from the desert, from a dreary mountainous region near Jerusalem, called Tekoa. Even if he wore his best, his clothes must have been plain and rough. His hair could not have been oiled or fashionably curled. His skin was dark and weather-beaten. In Tekoa, he

tended sheep and took care of sycamore trees. Perhaps when he came to the city to sell his wool and the fig-like fruit of the sycamore tree, he saw how great a difference there was between the rich and the poor. When he returned to the simple life of the desert and watched his sheep under the open sky, he wondered if there should be such differences between men. At last he could not help himself. He had to open his lips to prophesy.

The message which Amos brought to Israel had three parts. Again and again he emphasized one central thought. God was not a God of one nation, but the Lord of the entire world—a universal God. Moab and Egypt, Phoenicia and Ammon, Judah and Israel, were all separate nations, but one God watched over them. He would teach them the way to happiness. He would punish them for their sins. All men were the children of one God.

Amos also said that God's greatest desire was for men to be just, fair, and kind to each other. A sacrifice could not make up for a wrong deed.

Lastly, Amos saw that there was trouble coming from the north, from the powerful kingdom of Assyria, which was growing stronger and greedier for land and power, year by year. He warned the people to be alert to this danger. If they were not divided into two groups of rich and poor, they would be better able to unite when the time came.

The priests, the nobles, and the king did not listen to Amos. They did not change their ways. He went back to Tekoa. He had done all he could do for Israel.

Amos was not the only prophet who spoke at that time. Hosea, an Israelite, also prophesied. Hosea was a man who had suffered a great deal in his life. He wanted to save his people from suffering. His words were kind and gentle. He told the people that God loved them as a father loves a child, and pleaded with them to stop their evil ways. Hosea, too, went unheeded. There were only a few who listened to him and to Amos. The others were proud and haughty. They believed that Israel was so strong and so rich that no country would dare to oppose it.

While Jeroboam II lived, all was well. But the story of Israel was soon to change.

SOMETHING TO TALK OVER IN CLASS

How could divisions of very rich and very poor come about at a time when Israel was prosperous?

What prophet might have said that God declared, "I am the Lord, thy God, and the God of Moab, of Egypt and of Phoenicia"?

What other ideas did the prophet ask the people of Israel to accept?

How did the Israelites treat him?

What other prophet spoke in Israel at this time?

What did he emphasize in his message?

WRITE A STORY ABOUT ONE OF THESE TOPICS

How an Israelite lost all his possessions in a bad year.

Amos at the steps of the temple in Bethel.

READ

In the Land of Kings and Prophets by Schwarz, pp. 89–95.

The Voice of the Prophets by Mamie G. Gamoran
   "God's Love for Israel," p. 134.

Stories of the Prophets by Isaac Landman, pp. 3–47.

19. A KINGDOM IS LOST

ONLY TWO years after Jeroboam II died, the good years which Israel had enjoyed began to come to an end. Once again there were struggles for the throne and the king did not feel secure.

Assyria, the sleeping giant of the north, had awakened. She had conquered her neighbor, Babylonia, and now looked for more power and more land. She was the ruler of the entire Mesopotamian region. Now she wished to extend her rule farther and farther. Down the coast of the Mediterranean Sea lay the proud country of Egypt. By conquering Egypt, Assyria would be mistress of the ancient world. It seemed easy. Only little kingdoms, like Aram, Israel, Judah, and Tyre stood in the way.

In Israel King Menahem was told, "Fight Assyria! Egypt will help you." Could he trust Egypt to help? He decided his country was not ready to challenge its mighty enemy. He sent a huge gift to the king of Assyria. Assyria held back its plan of conquest. Israel remained at peace.

The times changed. Menahem died and his son was killed by a general in the army, named Pekah, who became king. Pekah was bolder than Menahem. He refused to send tribute to Assyria. He believed that if all the small kingdoms united, they could throw off the heavy hand of Assyria. Once more messages came from Egypt urging him to break with Assyria. Pekah united with the king of Aram. Even together, they did not feel strong enough to face Assyria. They determined to force Judah to join them. With an army, they rode down to Jerusalem. Perhaps this show of arms would win the support of the Judean king, named Ahaz.

Can you see the difficult position in which Ahaz found himself? He was sure that Assyria would conquer Israel and Aram. What difference would his puny force make in such a war? He longed to keep his land in peace. But Israel and Aram were on their way! Ahaz hit upon an unhappy plan. He sent messengers to ask the Assyrians for help.

Soon the mighty Assyrian army was on the march. The kings of Israel and Aram had to flee from Judah to save their kingdoms. Though their forces were united, they were not strong enough. The Assyrians took Damascus and then they marched on to Israel. King Pekah was killed and the entire northern part of Israel was overrun by the Assyrian army. Cities were ruined and their inhabitants were sent off to exile.

Israel was smaller than it had been, but it was still a nation with a new king. He was named Hoshea. At first, he too sent his tribute to Assyria. But when a new king came to that throne, hope rose again in the hearts of the conquered nations. Egypt urged them on with promises of help. Hoshea stopped paying his tribute. The small nations revolted. Shalmaneser IV, the new Assyrian king, came down with his army. He besieged Samaria, the capital of Israel. There were brave men in Samaria. For three years the city held out all alone. Egypt forgot its promises. No help came from anywhere. At last in

the year 722 B.C.E., the Assyrians broke down the walls of the city and entered.

The Assyrians were cruel conquerors. They burned the cities and tore through the countryside. They looted the fine homes of the rich merchants and farmers. They burned the grain in the barns and in the fields. All the wealth of the country went to Assyria. The people were exiled. Families were separated and sent far from their native land. Where they went, no one knows. They were scattered over all the lands which Assyria held. They were lost to their people. From that time on they were called the Lost Ten Tribes of Israel.

You have surely heard many stories and legends about the Lost Ten Tribes. Some tell that they live in a far-off land, guarded by a strange river, the Sambatyon. Day and night, all through the week, the Sambatyon rushes along its course, throwing up great rocks as it goes. None can pass over the river on these days. Only on the Sabbath is the river quiet, but no one would enter the land on the day of rest. So, undiscovered and undisturbed, says the legend, the Ten Tribes still live beyond the Sambatyon.

When America was discovered, some writers declared that the Indians were descendants of the Lost Ten Tribes, and among the English people there was a legend that their ancestors were the fabled people of the land of Israel.

A new group of people from other conquered lands was sent into Israel. Later, some of them became known as Samaritans, after the name of the capital. Perhaps a few priests still remained in the country, hidden away with a few Israelites who had escaped the sharp eyes of the Assyrian soldiers. In time, the newcomers learned some of the laws and some of the practices of the religion of Israel. We shall hear about the Samaritans later on.

The kingdom of Israel existed about two hundred and ten years. During that time there were years when it was very small. Early in its history under Omri, and later under Jeroboam II, it was one of the great powers of its time. Although at times its people added foreign gods and idols to their shrines, they always worshipped the God of the Hebrews and sacrificed to Him.

From the pages of Israel's stormy history emerged great, never-to-be-forgotten figures. First came the early prophets like Elijah and Elisha. They feared no one and devoted themselves to the task of keeping the people faithful to their ancient religion. After them appeared the first of the literary prophets, Amos, who begged the people to worship God not only by sacrifice but also by good deeds. On the soil of Israel, for the first time, voices were heard demanding justice and fair-dealing for the poor and the oppressed. The beautiful picture of God as a loving Father who longs to forgive His child came from Hosea, another of Israel's prophets. From this small nation the idea went forth of a universal God who is not held by the boundaries of a country, but who watches over all men in all countries. Israel vanished from the scene of history, but the words of her prophets lived on.

QUESTIONS TO TALK OVER IN CLASS

What prophet first saw the shadow of the conqueror coming over Israel?

What kings united against a common foe?

Whom did they ask to join them?

In what year did Israel fall? How long did it exist?

Why can the little land of Israel never be forgotten by the world?

Was it better for Ahaz to keep peace in Judah or to help Israel?

WRITE

A story or poem about the Ten Lost Tribes.

READ

In the Land of Kings and Prophets by Schwarz, pp. 105–108.

Hillel's Happy Holidays by Mamie G. Gamoran
    "A River that Rests," p. 11.

Lost Worlds by White
    "In the Bosom of Kuyunjik," pp. 196–200.

The Lore of the Old Testament by Gaer
    "The Eye of the Mind," p. 274.

Unit 7

Great Ideas in a Small Land

You begin this unit by making a journey to the land of Judah and paying a visit to its most important city. Do you think you would have enjoyed living there at that time?

Like Israel, Judah was forging its claims to a place in world history. Its prophets spoke words of wisdom and beauty; its priests wrote down its early history, and in its last days its kings brought the people back to the laws and religion which was theirs alone.

No more exciting pages in history can be found than these which follow, dealing with the last days of the kingdom of Judah.

The Busy Market-Place

20. DAY BY DAY

EVEN WHEN kings were busy with problems of war, while messengers traveled with laden donkeys carrying tributes of gold and gifts of cunning jewelry to foreign rulers, and while prophets spoke in market-places and temple steps about God and man, the ordinary life of most people went on from day to day.

So it was in Judah. The people knew what had happened to Israel. Some of the families of Israel must have fled southward to Judah where they may have had friends or relatives. The men and women of Judah heard their stories and helped them to begin life again. There was not very much difference between the life of the Israelites and the Judeans. Israel had several important cities and carried on more trade with foreign countries, but in both lands farmers toiled on the soil, shepherds watched their flocks, priests served in the Temple in Jerusalem and in the smaller shrines in the villages, merchants bought and sold the goods of the land and of foreign traders, and all hoped that the king with his advisers would manage the political affairs of the country to keep them in peace.

Judah had led a fairly peaceful existence since the division of the kingdom. There had been some warfare with neighboring cities and even with Israel, but those years of war were the exception, not the rule. A descendant of David still ruled in Jerusalem, even though he held his throne by paying tribute to Assyria.

The most important city in the land of Judah was Jerusalem. It was surrounded by a strong wall with many entrances or gates. At night the gates would be closed and no one could enter or leave until the next morning.

During the day the gates were busy places. At the entrance, people were coming and going. Around the gates were the market-places, thronged with buyers, sellers, and idlers who came to watch what was going on.

Jerusalem was not as large or magnificent as some of the cities of Egypt or Assyria, but the Judeans loved and admired it. To them, the Temple with its inner and outer courts, and the palace of the king surrounded by houses for his wives, his servants, and his soldiers seemed very grand.

When a countryman came to Jerusalem, he was pleased and satisfied with what he saw. If he entered at the main gate, he might see a large caravan of Egyptians coming in on camels,

with donkeys carrying heavy loads of goods to sell. Perhaps an important messenger from the Pharaoh would come with the caravan, riding on a richly decorated camel. The country-man would wander around the markets and see goods from other countries waiting to be sold. Each market had its own name and had its own specialties. There was the leather mar-ket, the wool market or the spice market. In the large bazaars one could buy anything, jewelry, perfumes, fine hangings, spices, curious foods, even furniture would be displayed. The wealthy city merchants or the nobles were ready to buy these articles to decorate their homes or to bring as gifts to their wives and daughters.

There were goods for the poorer buyers, too. The Judeans made their own pottery, their own water flasks and cook-ing vessels, and these were cheap enough for anyone. They sheared the wool from their sheep and dyed it into bright col-ors. Then the women wove it into cloth for clothing and for coverings for floors and walls. Some clever Judean workmen had learned to copy from the foreign merchants and could make fine articles like jewelry or embroidered cloths to sell in the market-place.

Just inside the gates, there was always something interest-ing going on. On a raised platform, judges would sit and listen to complaints. Those who had time gathered around to listen to the men who brought their affairs to be settled. The judges would not take long to decide who was right and who was wrong, and the crowds would wait around to hear the judg-ment.

A band of prophets might pass by and one of their company would stop and call to the crowd to listen to him. He might

stand before a booth which had wooden idols and household gods for sale and scold the people for buying them. Poor men, who had no land and no business, stood around waiting to hire out for a day's work, and somewhere in the market would be a place where slaves were sold. It did not seem strange or wrong to own slaves at that time. It was the practice in every land. One of the rewards of war was the number of slaves who were captured. However, the Torah, even that part which was written in very early times, had many rules to control the treatment of slaves. The Judeans were told to treat their slaves kindly and not harshly. According to the law, a Judean who sold himself or his children into slavery for payment of a debt was freed after six years. The law also said that a master who bought such a slave should "treat him as a brother." In time, the slave could buy his freedom. A master was not permitted to injure or kill his slaves, whether they were Judeans or foreigners. All slaves were freed at the Jubilee year which came every fifty years. We believe that on the whole these rules were faithfully carried out, and we are glad that the peo-

ple of Judah were taught to be kind and fair to their slaves.

The markets were not the only places where men could gain a livelihood. Builders had learned to put up large and comfortable stone houses for the well-to-do city people. Iron workers made spears and arrows for the soldiers to carry. With crude instruments, engineers arranged for a supply of water for the city. Priests and Levites had their duties in the Temple and received gifts when they performed a sacrifice.

Along the narrow streets of the city rose the one- or two-story stone houses. The roofs were flat-topped and families would spend much of their free time there, especially in the evening when it was cooler on the roofs than in the houses. Some of the richer people had larger houses with many rooms, and paved or cobbled courtyards. In these homes, against the rich hangings, or in a corner of the room, there often could be found small household idols. Although some of the Judeans kept heathen idols in their homes, they brought offerings to the Temple and worshipped there. No one went to Jerusalem without visiting the Temple and passing by the king's palace. In this part of the city the streets were wider and paved with cobblestones.

Only sons of wealthy families went to school. The other boys and girls in Jerusalem and in the rest of the country did not go to classes. Boys usually learned their father's profession or trade. A man who was a weaver taught his son to be a weaver, and a merchant's son would learn all about his father's business. The priests and Levites, we know, came from the tribe of Levi, and handed their positions down for generations from father to son. A father was supposed to teach his son the rules of right and wrong and also the prayers and songs he had learned from his father. It was important to have a good memory, for this instruction was usually not in writing. It was probably given in odd moments when there was no work to be done. Only priests and some important merchants and nobles could read and write. Some men wrote letters and copied records. They were called scribes. A girl learned household tasks, such as cooking, spinning, and weaving from her mother.

Clothes were simple. Nearly everyone wore a long robe called a simlah, tied around the middle with a girdle, a head-covering of some sort against the burning sun, and sandals on his feet. Children ran barefoot. Wealthy people had their robes made of finely woven cloth, and the girdles were embroidered and jeweled, while a poor man or a slave had only a coarse garment to cover him.

Outside the city, in the little towns and villages, lived the families of the farmers and the shepherds. The men came to the city only to sell their wares. Their goods were grain, oil, fruit and vegetables, poultry, eggs and cheese, wool, and woven goods. In the city markets they would sell or exchange what they had for other goods they needed.

Country homes were not as fine as city houses. Usually they were built of bricks made of dried mud. A farmer with even a small piece of land or a shepherd with a small flock lived a simple but comfortable life. It was only when bad years brought a famine, and a man lost his land because of debts, that poverty came to the countryside. In this way, some men became very rich with large estates and others had nothing.

Most villages had an altar or shrine where priests who passed through would pray and make sacrifices. The villagers might sometimes place an idol in these shrines, an image of a Canaanite or Mesopotamian god. If one of the members of a wandering band of prophets came to the village and saw the idol, he would become angry and destroy it. Then he would beg the villagers to pray to the God of Israel and not to a wooden or stone image.

This was the way the people of Judah lived for hundreds of years. They had changed gradually from tent-dwellers and wanderers to settled city and country folk. Some families had begun to live in luxury; some had fallen into slavery. They had learned many things from their neighbors, and were slowly beginning to learn important lessons from their leaders and their prophets. These lessons would later be heard in other lands far from the little country of Judah.

SOMETHING TO WRITE ABOUT

Imagine you are a country boy or girl on a visit to Jerusalem. Write a composition describing your visit.

Imagine you are an Israelite who escaped from the Assyrian soldiers. Write a story about how you fled from Samaria to Jerusalem and found safety in the home of your cousin.

Imagine you are a priest and you found someone selling idols. Write out the speech you would make to the people in the market-place.

SOMETHING TO DO TOGETHER

Find out if any of the children in school have been to Israel. If not, a mother or father, an aunt or uncle may have visited there. Try to borrow some clothes, some objects, or some pictures which would remind you of earlier times. Arrange an exhibit of Israel, old and new, and invite some of the other classes to see it.

READ

> *Down Holiday Lane* by Golub
> "Sukos in Ancient Palestine," p. 18.
> *A Picture Book of Palestine* by Smither, pp. 5–44.

READINGS FOR TEACHERS

Unit VII (*CHAPTERS 20–23*)

The Bible, Isaiah 1–39.

The Jews, Chap. I, pp. 41–48.

A History of the Jewish People by Margolis and Marx, Chaps. XVIII–XXI.

Preface to Scripture, Part Two, by Freehof, Chap. V, pp. 103–114, 121–131; Chap. VI, pp. 167–177.

Life of the People in Bible Times by Radin. Chapters on Education, City and Country, and Occupations are especially valuable at this time.

21. THE WISE PROPHET

IT IS the habit of kings to write down their accomplishments to show their might and their glory. In ancient days, they left carvings on monuments, on statues and sometimes even on rocks to tell of their great deeds. It is lucky for us, who are trying to learn of those bygone days, that they did so. More and more of these carvings are being discovered to tell us exciting stories of long ago.

In 1880, a young English boy living in Palestine noticed a rock with an ancient Hebrew inscription carved into the hard stone. Scholars got to work to read and translate the inscription. It told how, almost 2,700 years ago, a tunnel was dug from the village of Siloam outside of Jerusalem to bring water into the city. The inscription described the exciting moment when two gangs of workmen coming from both sides of the tunnel could hear each other's pickaxes ringing through the rock wall that separated them. Just a few more blows and the tunnel would be completed. Even today, you can see the place in the tunnel where the two gangs met. The marks of the pickaxes still show how the men were working from two directions.

This tunnel, according to the Bible, was dug in the days of Hezekiah, king of Judah, to bring water into Jerusalem if an

enemy stood outside the walls and prevented the people from
going out for water. When it was finished the king was proud
to have his workmen carve the story on a rock for men to read
for thousands of years to come.

Why was Hezekiah fearful that an enemy might threaten
the city of Jerusalem?

The little kingdom of Judah passed through a stormy period
after Israel fell. The same problems which had troubled Israel
now faced her. From many sides came bribes, bargains,
threats.

Egypt, Aram, Assyria, each called to her in turn. The kings
of Judah were perplexed and troubled. To whom could they
turn for advice?

You would think that the ruler would have a prime minister
or a great lord for his adviser. No—at this time the monarchs
of the southern kingdom turned to Isaiah, the great prophet
of Judah.

Isaiah was different from the prophets you have met so far. He was born of a noble family and was well received in the court. His words were listened to by the greatest in the land—by the king, nobles and priests—although they were not always heeded. Isaiah is called a statesman, a man who carefully watched the events not only of his own country but of its neighbors. He understood how the actions of these nations affected his own land. This made his advice clear, wise, and valuable. He lived and spoke during the reigns of Uzziah, Jotham, Ahaz, and Hezekiah—four kings of Judah.

The Book of Isaiah in the Bible has sixty-six chapters. Scholars believe that the first thirty-nine were written by Isaiah of Judah. It is his story we are telling now. The other twenty-seven chapters were written by an unknown prophet who is also called Isaiah. He prophesied later in another land. You will hear more about him in another chapter.

Isaiah's prophecies are of two kinds, religious and political. Sometimes he spoke of the injustice he found in the land. Sometimes his words were words of guidance to the king.

When Ahaz heard that the kings of Israel and Aram wanted him to join them in a revolt against Assyria, he turned to Isaiah for advice. Isaiah told him to be calm and to do nothing. He did not want Judah to become involved in wars with other countries. Ahaz did not listen to the prophet. He sent gold and gifts to the king of Assyria and asked for help. You know now how Assyria invaded Aram and Israel. This was the beginning of the destruction of Israel.

Thus Judah became a vassal country of Assyria. Every year she had to pay a huge tribute. The grain, the wool, the sheep, and the gold that formed the tribute came not only from the wealthy families. The poor farmers, shepherds, and artisans who labored for them had a heavy share of the burden. Once more, as in Israel in the days of Amos and Hosea, there were poverty and suffering on the one hand, greed and injustice on the other. Isaiah spoke against these evils to the rich and powerful men in the land. He reminded them of their duty to their people and to their religion. He raised his voice against the oppression of the poor. He cried out:

> Cease to do evil;
> Learn to do well;
> Seek justice, relieve the oppressed,
> Judge the fatherless, plead for the
>   widow.

Again he told the people, as Amos had done, that God does not look for sacrifices as much as for good deeds. His words were:

> To what purpose is the multitude of your
>   sacrifices unto Me?
> Saith, the Lord;
> I am full of the burnt-offerings of rams,
> And the fat of fed beasts;
> And I delight not in the blood
> Of bullocks, or of lambs, or of he-goats.

Many changes could be seen in the land. Ahaz visited the king of Assyria, Tiglath-Pileser. To show how much he respected the new master of Judah, the king brought back a pattern for a new altar and placed it in the Temple, together with new Assyrian gods to worship. The priests were ordered to follow the new ways of worship which the king brought in. Isaiah pleaded for a return to the religion of Israel. From his words

we learn that there was still idol-worship in Judah, especially
on the part of the wealthy group.

> Their land also is full of silver and gold,
> Neither is there any end of their treasures;
> Their land also is full of idols;
> Every one worshippeth the work of his
>   own hands.

Isaiah's words were not always stern and forbidding. Again
and again he told of God's love for Israel. God will not desert
His people. No matter what happens He would save a part, a
remnant, and bring them back to their land.

> And it shall come to pass in that day,
> That the Lord will set His hand again . . .
> To recover the remnant of His peo-
>   ple, . . .
> And will assemble the dispersed of Israel,
> And gather together the scattered of Judah
> From the four corners of the earth.

The Book of Isaiah is so full of beautiful passages that it is im-
possible to tell you of all of them. The prophet believed that
the city of Jerusalem could never be destroyed. We have seen

that this prophecy has come true. Jerusalem, high on the hill
of Zion, has been the Holy City for men and women all over
the world for thousands of years. From the mountain of the
Lord, said Isaiah, would come knowledge of God, justice, and
peace for the world.

> And it shall come to pass in the end of days,
> That the mountain of the Lord's house shall
>   be established as the top of the moun-
>   tains,
> And shall be exalted above the hills;
> And all nations shall flow unto it.
> And many peoples shall go and say:
> "Come ye and let us go up to the mountain
>   of the Lord,
> To the house of the God of Jacob;
> And He will teach us of His ways,
> And we will walk in His paths."
> For out of Zion shall go forth the law,
> And the word of the Lord from Jerusalem.
> And he shall judge between the nations,
> And shall decide for many peoples;
> And they shall beat their swords into plow-
>   shares,
> And their spears into pruning-hooks;
> Nation shall not lift up sword against nation,
> Neither shall they learn war any more.

Isaiah's hope was that Judah was not to be a nation seeking
wealth and large territory. It would show its greatness when
it became a nation whose people followed in the paths of
justice, loved God, and performed His commandments.

Isaiah believed that Judah would continue to be ruled by
descendants of David. He had a vision of the future, when one
of David's descendants would rule the land with justice and

judge righteously. "In that day," said Isaiah, "the earth shall
be full of the knowledge of the Lord, as the waters over
the sea."

To save his beloved land, Isaiah once prophesied in an unusual way. The time came when Hezekiah, the new king of
Judah, wished to be free of the Assyrians. He listened to
Egypt who promised to help if the small nations banded together against Assyria. Isaiah did not trust Egypt. One day
the people of Jerusalem were astonished to see Isaiah on the
streets. For this time it was not Isaiah as they usually met him,
well-dressed and clean, but Isaiah, half-naked and barefoot, as
though he were being taken captive to Assyria. To the crowds
that gathered around he cried:

> Woe to them that go down to Egypt for
>   help, . . .
> And trust in chariots, because they are many,
> And in horsemen because they are mighty,
> But they look not unto the Holy One of
>   Israel,
> Neither seek out the Lord.

He begged the king not to break with Assyria and to trust in the Lord.

Before long the king saw how wise Isaiah had been. Not far away was the city of Ashdod. It rebelled against Assyria. It was destroyed and all its people were taken captive.

As Isaiah's words were so dramatically proven true, the people began to heed them. The king ordered the Temple cleansed of Assyrian idols. He sent messengers throughout the land to seek out small shrines and places of worship where idols were to be found. They were all destroyed. Jerusalem was once more set up as the central place of worship. Hezekiah held a service in the purified Temple. The priests offered sacrifices to make atonement for the sins of the people. The Levites played on the cymbals and the harps and the psalteries. Singers sang songs of praise and of thanksgiving. The service became known as Hezekiah's rededication of the Temple. People came from the little towns and villages near Jeru-

salem to hear the service. They were told that Passover was coming and were reminded to observe their ancient feast of freedom. Even the few Israelites who were still in the land of Israel were invited to come to Jerusalem for the Passover feast. During Hezekiah's reign, the priests and the people faithfully carried out the commandments of their religion.

Hezekiah's faith in Isaiah was again put to the test a few years later. This time Babylonia urged the king not to pay his tribute to the Assyrians. Hezekiah agreed. Sennacherib, the king of Assyria, in all his might, with chariots, horses and footmen, came against his rebelling provinces. One by one they fell before him. Hezekiah was forced to pay a huge tribute. Sennacherib asked more. He was determined to have the city of Jerusalem. Hezekiah came to Isaiah, the prophet who spoke in God's name. What would he advise now?

This time Isaiah had words of encouragement for the troubled king. Assyria was too proud, he said; she would fall. He believed that Assyria was only the rod of God who had been angry with His people for their wicked ways. God had used the rod to punish Israel for its sins. Now Assyria would be punished in turn. Isaiah told the leaders not to fear. His words were clear and forceful:

> Thus saith the Lord concerning the king of Assyria:
> He shall not come into this city, nor shoot an arrow there,
> Neither shall he come before it with shield.

Sennacherib's men were encamped about the walls of Jerusalem. At any moment they would storm the city. Who could believe that Isaiah's words would come true?

But a ruler who tries to conquer the world has many difficulties. A revolt broke out at home in Nineveh. Sennacherib was forced to give up the siege and prepare to return to Assyria. While the astonished guards watched from their towers on Jerusalem's walls, the Assyrian soldiers suddenly departed. In addition, a great plague broke out among the Assyrian soldiers and many of them died.

Judah was saved. The king reigned in Jerusalem, though tribute still went to Assyria.

Ahaz and Hezekiah reigned for about forty years. During all that time, Isaiah spoke to them, scolded them, and encouraged them. With his help Jerusalem became the strong center both of government and religion. He influenced the wealthy to become kinder and more just to the poor and caused many reforms to be made by the priests in worship and sacrifice. Like Amos, he spoke of God as the Lord of all the nations, not only of Israel and Judah.

Isaiah was statesman, poet, and prophet. By following his wise counsel his country came through a difficult period safely.

There was another prophet who lived and spoke at this time. He was very different from Isaiah. His name was Micah and he was a peasant who lived in a village near Gath, the Philistine city. It is possible that Micah saw how the Assyrians swept down on Samaria and drove its inhabitants far away. He believed that Israel had been punished for its idolatry and for the injustice that was found within its borders. He called out against injustice and evil. Like the other prophets he declared that God does not look only for sacrifices and offerings. Very clearly and simply, he told the people what God asked of all men. Micah said:

It hath been told thee, O man, what is good,
And what the Lord doth require of thee:
Only to do justly, and to love mercy, and to
    walk humbly with thy God.

Twenty-seven hundred years have passed since Micah lived
in his little village. In all this time, no one has expressed this
thought in more beautiful words or in a way that is easier to
understand.

SOMETHING TO TALK OVER IN CLASS

Who prophesied during the reign of four kings?
Tell a story of a king who did not follow his advice.
Tell of one who did.
Was Isaiah the only prophet who spoke at this time?
If not, name the other prophet. Give a line from his prophecy
that is quoted very often.

READ

The Voice of the Prophets by Gamoran
"The Vision of the Future," p. 6,
"What Doth God Require?" p. 190.
(Turn to page 7. Then turn to page 188. What do you find? Are
you surprised?)
Stories of the Prophets by Landman
"The Commoner," pp. 135–149.
The Burning Bush by Gaer
"The Battle That Wasn't Fought," p. 294.

22. A BOOK THAT MADE HISTORY

DATES in a history book usually mark a battle, the death of a king, or the conquest of a territory. The date 621 B.C.E. commemorates none of these, yet is one of the most important dates in Jewish history. In that year, when young King Josiah was on the throne of Judah, a book was discovered. How can the finding of a book be so important? Let us try to find out.

During the long reign of Manesseh, the son of Hezekiah, Judah was a vassal of Assyria. Tribute went regularly from Jerusalem to Nineveh. Once, Judean troops were even sent to help Assyria fight Egypt. Messengers must have been going back and forth between the two lands. It is not surprising to learn that once again Assyrian gods and idols were brought into Jerusalem and placed in the Temple. The shrines and high places that Hezekiah had destroyed were rebuilt and priests, as in the years gone by, deserted their ancient faith and practiced the religion of the rulers of the land. Foreign rulers seemed to mean that foreign worship was brought into a country.

Josiah was different from his grandfather, Manasseh, who copied the Assyrians in every way. Perhaps it was because he dreamed of making Judah independent once again. Two prophets named Nahum and Zephaniah had foretold the doom of Assyria and hopes ran high for freedom. Perhaps it was because of the words of a young prophet, Jeremiah, who came to Jerusalem and spoke against idolatry and injustice and evil. Many people listened to his words; they were sons and grandsons of the men who had listened to Isaiah, the sons and grandsons of the priests who had followed out Hezekiah's orders, and descendants of the men and women who had attended the great service at the Temple years before. Quietly they worked and waited, writing down the great prophecies of Isaiah and Micah. They hoped that the new king would listen to them and not to foreign priests who prayed to idols, who sometimes sacrificed children, whose religion did not insist that men be good and kind to each other.

Josiah's unknown teachers were successful. He ordered the Temple prepared and cleaned. One day, in the year 621 B.C.E., the workers made an important discovery. Somewhere in a dark corner of the Temple, a Scroll of the Law was found.

This was no ordinary scroll, but one that seemed to be very ancient and was said to be written by the great lawgiver himself, by Moses. Hilkiah, the High Priest, came to the palace to read the new-found book to the monarch.

This scroll, we know now, was part of the Book of Deuteronomy, the fifth book of the Torah. It must have been written by someone hidden away, in the days when it was not safe to fight openly against idol-worship. Deuteronomy is a book of laws, with rules for worship and behavior, but it is not just a list of laws to be obeyed and rules to be followed. Its language is almost like the language of the prophets, poetic and stirring. It is filled with a wonderful feeling of God's love for man. The people were told to carry out the laws which Moses gave them because they loved God, not because they feared Him. There are many verses like these, "Rejoice before the Lord thy God" or "Thou shalt be altogether joyful."

Deuteronomy thundered against idolatry. We read, "Know this day, and lay it to thy heart, that the Lord, He is God in heaven above and upon the earth beneath; there is none else."

Many passages in Deuteronomy will be familiar to you, for this book is the foundation of some of the most wonderful ideals of the Jewish people. You will recognize, "Hear, O Israel: the Lord our God, the Lord is one," which is taken from the sixth chapter of the scroll. This watchword of the Jewish people is followed by the words which you have read in the prayer book: "And thou shalt love the Lord thy God, with all thy heart, with all thy soul, and with all thy might."

Deuteronomy told again the story of the wanderings in the wilderness. It repeated many of the laws found in the second book of the Pentateuch, Exodus, including the Ten Com-

mandments. But there were changes in these laws. They are
kinder and more generous than they had been. The Judeans
were reminded that they were strangers and slaves in Egypt.
Therefore they were urged to be kind to strangers and slaves
in their midst. The book ends with two beautiful poems. The
last few lines describe the death of Moses, the beloved leader
of his people.

When we read parts of Deuteronomy, we almost believe
that the unknown writer knew what was in store for his people—knew that they would some day be separated from their
land. For over and over again, the beauty of the land was described. The people were told that if they obeyed the commandments of Moses, God would bless them and also their
land. It would be fruitful and bring forth "corn and wine
and oil."

The command, "Justice, justice shalt thou pursue," is also
found in this book. It is no wonder that when Josiah heard the
impressive words of Deuteronomy, they struck deep into his
heart. He determined that once again he would clear the land
of Assyrian priests, of idols and of false shrines. He vowed to
make his people hear the words of Moses which seemed to
come like an echo from the past, guiding their footsteps.

Josiah needed advice. He turned to Huldah who, like Deborah, is called a prophetess in the Bible. We do not have any
of her writings, but we are told that she hurried to the king to
give him a message. She told him that God would forgive the
people of Judah if they turned to Him again.

Josiah was encouraged. He called the people to a great assembly at the Temple. There on a platform he stood in the
midst of priests, nobles, townsmen, and farmers. To them he

read the words which Moses was supposed to have said many years earlier.

"Ye are standing this day all of you before the Lord your God; your heads, your tribes, your elders, and your officers, even all the men of Israel, your little ones, your wives and the stranger that is in the midst of thy camp . . . that thou should enter into the covenant of the Lord thy God, which the Lord thy God maketh with thee this day; that He may establish thee this day unto Himself for a people, and that He may be unto thee a God . . . as He swore unto thy fathers, to Abraham, to Isaac and to Jacob."

What a scene that must have been as Josiah read and called on the people to follow the laws of Deuteronomy! What a revolution it brought about! The people were filled with zeal.

Messengers went throughout the land, destroying the idols and the shrines which had been erected. Even as far north as Bethel, which was once in Israel, they went, bringing the new law. Jerusalem was established as the great center of religious life, and as the holy city. The laws of kindness of every man to his fellow man were proclaimed throughout the land.

All this unified the people and knit them together. A loyal and patriotic Judean loved his religion and his land. When the ancient tradition was followed, and a great Passover celebration was held later in the year, the Judeans felt that they would soon be blessed with God's favor and perhaps their land would be free.

It is true that Judah was very small, but Josiah was slowly regaining some of the territory which had been lost to the invaders, and was even reaching up to the boundaries of Israel.

In 612 something happened which shook the ancient world. The Assyrian capital, Nineveh, fell to a great army from the south. Assyria met the fate which it had decreed for so many other nations—it disappeared. A new power, the Chaldeans or Babylonians, began to take their place in history.

Once again a prophet's words were fulfilled. Nahum, who lived at this time, had said:

> Behold upon the mountains the feet of him
> That bringeth good tidings, that announc-
>   eth peace!
> Keep thy feasts, O Judah,
> Perform thy vows;
> For the wicked one shall no more pass
>   through thee;
> He is utterly cut off.

He described how the Assyrian horsemen and chariots would rush hither and thither but would not be able to escape their fate. He continued:

> Thy shepherds slumber, O king
>   of Assyria,
> Thy worthies are at rest;
> Thy people are scattered upon
>   the mountains,
> And there is none to gather them.
> There is no assuaging of thy hurt,
> Thy wound is grievous;
> All that hear the report of thee
> Clap the hands over thee;
> For upon whom hath not thy
>   wickedness passed continually.

No, there was none to weep over the fall of Assyria.

The nations all around were in a state of great excitement. The little countries hoped for freedom. The large kingdoms dreamed of conquest.

Egypt decided to send an army north to help Assyria fight the Babylonians. The way led across Judah. Josiah had strengthened his land. His people loved him and were ready to follow him. This was his chance to free his country. He decided to prevent the Egyptians from marching through Judah. At a battle-field near the city of Megiddo, the two forces clashed. But almost at once Josiah was killed by an arrow. The battle was lost.

The good years of Josiah's reign came to a sudden end. However, the work he had done was not forgotten. He accepted the great Book of Deuteronomy and made it known to the people. He strengthened the hands of the small group which had remained faithful to the words of the prophets. Through them the future of the Jewish people was made secure.

QUESTIONS TO TALK OVER IN CLASS

Read the Ten Commandments in Exodus, Chapter 20 and in Deuteronomy, Chapter 5. Did you find any differences?

How did a foreign ruler show his power over conquered lands? Did he ask more than just paying tribute?

Can you think of a modern country which forces its ideas on lands which it controls?

Should we teach backward countries modern ways of living? How should this be done?

READ

Stories of the Prophets by Landman
"The Great Discovery," pp. 180–193.
Great Jewish Women by Levinger
"Huldah, a Teacher in Israel," pp. 59–61.

23. WHEN JUDAH FELL

IN A small village called Anathoth, not far from Jerusalem, a son was born to one of the well-to-do priestly families. The parents called their son Jeremiah. The boy was well educated and in his early years lived quietly in the village with his family.

As a young man, Jeremiah felt that God called upon him to prophesy. In the Book of Jeremiah he wrote that God said to him, "I have appointed thee a prophet unto the nations."

Jeremiah replied: "Ah, Lord God, I cannot speak, for I am a child." Of course he was no longer a child, but he did not think he was old enough to prophesy.

The answer came:

> Say not: I am a child;
> Whatsoever I shall command thee
>   thou shalt speak.
> Be not afraid of them;
> For I am with thee to deliver thee,
> Saith the Lord.

Once again, we see clearly what moved a prophet to speak. He was carrying out God's will to bring His words to his fellow men. Jeremiah accepted the task. For forty years he prophesied in Judah. They were years of trial and turmoil.

When Josiah was killed and the army defeated, his son became king. He reigned only three months when he was removed from the throne by Egypt. His brother was put in his place. He was loyal to Egypt and its ways. To pay the great tribute which Egypt demanded, huge taxes were taken from the people. Even more money was forced from them to build a new palace for the king.

Jeremiah spoke against putting such heavy loads on the poor. He warned that wickedness be punished. His life was in danger many times. Once his writings were seized by the king and burned to ashes. But he was not frightened. He continued to speak:

> For among my people are found wicked men,
> They plead not the cause, the cause of the
>   fatherless,
> That they might make it to prosper,
> And the right of the needy do they not judge.
> Shall I not punish, saith the Lord,
> Shall not My soul be avenged
> On such a nation as this?

He too, like the prophets before him, declared that sacrifice which did not come from the heart had no meaning. He called on the people to follow their ancient laws—not only to bring offerings to the altars.

> Your burnt offerings are not acceptable,
> Nor your sacrifices pleasing to Me.

In the midst of political unrest a prophet did not forget that the most important thing in a nation's life was the well-being of its people. To extend the borders of the land was good, but to see that all men were treated justly was an even greater task for the king and his followers.

The struggle for power among the large nations continued. Egypt fell before Babylonia which grew stronger and stronger. For a short time Judah paid tribute to Nebuchadnezzar, king of Babylonia. Then the king rebelled and stopped his tribute, thinking that Nebuchadnezzar was too busy in other places to pay attention to the little country of Judah.

All this Jeremiah saw and warned against. He believed that Babylonia was too strong for Judah to defy. He spoke of a vision of the future when all the people of Judah would make a new covenant with God to follow His laws and commandments. In this Judah would find her true strength. To be safe you must be righteous, Jeremiah told the people who assembled to hear him:

> If ye thoroughly amend your way and your doings; if ye thoroughly execute justice between a man and his neighbour; if ye oppress not the stranger, the fatherless, and the widow, . . . neither walk after other gods to your hurt; then will I cause you to dwell in this place, in the land that I gave to your fathers for ever and ever.

But Nebuchadnezzar kept his eye on his vassal states. He knew when Judah did not send its tribute. He came to the walls of Jerusalem with his army in the year 597 B.C.E. A new king, only eighteen years old, was now on the throne. What could he do but surrender? The Babylonians took many Judeans captive, and sent them into exile. Nebuchadnezzar picked the wealthy and educated men, the skilled workers, many priests and soldiers and sent them off to Babylonia.

Fortunately these men and their families were not scattered or persecuted in Babylonia. They were permitted to live safely in the city of Babylon and to follow their own religion. Letters and messengers went between Babylonia and Judea.

Jeremiah remained in Jerusalem. The new king, appointed by Nebuchadnezzar from the royal family, was named Zedekiah. His advisers kept urging him to revolt. Other small nations promised to help. "Do not rebel," cried Jeremiah. "Pay your tribute to Babylonia. Judah will be doomed if she rebels." The king was undecided.

One day the people of Jerusalem saw a strange sight. Through the streets of the city came Jeremiah. Around his shoulders he bore a heavy yoke, like the yoke of oxen. "Bear

the yoke of Babylonia," he declared. "It will save us from destruction."

In Babylonia, the exiles heard that revolution was in the air. They too secretly planned rebellion. Jeremiah wrote them a letter of advice. Many years later and in many different lands, Jews would read this letter in the Bible and in hard times they would be comforted.

> Build ye houses and dwell in them, and plant gardens and eat the fruit of them. And seek the peace of the city whither I have caused you to be carried away captive, and pray unto the Lord for it; for in the peace thereof shall ye have peace.

Jeremiah did not believe that the exile would last forever. He ended the letter by saying:

> After seventy years are accomplished for Babylon, I will remember you and perform My good word toward you in causing you to return to this place. For I know the thoughts I think towards you, saith the Lord, thoughts of peace and not of evil, to give you a future and a hope.

For ten years, Judah seesawed back and forth. To revolt or not to revolt. At last came a strong message from Egypt. If Judah rebelled, Egypt would send an army to fight by her side. This was the spark that touched off the rebellion. Jeremiah was thrown into prison to keep him from speaking.

Jerusalem prepared for a long siege. Its walls were strengthened. Food and water were stored. Nebuchadnezzar came with a huge army and camped outside the walls. The Jews looked for help from Egypt. Where was it? For months they bravely defended their city. But Nebuchadnezzar's battering-

rams struck the walls of the city day by day. At last Egypt's
soldiers did arrive. The Babylonians departed to give them
battle. But they were not gone long. Egypt's army had disappeared; the Babylonians returned. After twenty months of
siege the walls of the city were broken. On the ninth day of
Ov, in the year 586 B.C.E., Nebuchadnezzar and his army entered Jerusalem.

The Babylonians destroyed the city, burned the Temple,
and took thousands of Jews captive to Babylonia. There they
joined their brethren who had been exiled ten years before.

A book of the Bible tells the sad tale of the fall of Judah.
This is the Book of Lamentations which many scholars believe
may have been written by Jeremiah. In it, the writer pours out
his heart in beautiful poetry. Lamentations begins with the
well-known verses:

> How doth the city sit solitary,
> That was full of people!
> How is she become as a widow!
> She that was great among the nations,
> And princess among the provinces,
> How is she become tributary!

It describes the terror of the siege of the city and the ill-fortune that befell her inhabitants. However, in the midst of these sorrowful verses, the poet put in a note of hope. He said:

> For the Lord will not cast off for ever.
> For though He cause grief, yet will He
>   have compassion
> According to the multitude of His mercies.
> For He doth not afflict willingly,
> Nor grieve the children of men.

Lamentations expresses a deep love for Jerusalem and its people. In this great poem the writer makes clear his belief that even in exile there was hope for the future.

Most of the Jews remained in Judah. These were the very poorest farmers, herdsmen, and workers. Nebuchadnezzar appointed a governor to rule the land and sent him away from Jerusalem to a town called Mizpah. He gave Jeremiah his choice: to go with the exiles or to remain in Judah. Jeremiah did not wish to leave his beloved land. He remained with the governor, Gedaliah, during his short rule of five years. Again there was unrest in the land. Gedaliah was murdered and many Jews fled to Egypt. They took the aged prophet with them and he died on the strange soil of Egypt. Those who lived after him were to see his prophecies, both of destruction and of magnificent rebirth, fulfilled.

One hundred and thirty-six years had passed since Israel was destroyed. Judah's last years were troubled and stormy. Yet this period gave rise to some of the greatest literary masterpieces the world has known. The messages of the great prophets, Isaiah, Micah, and Jeremiah, together with the words of many others who prophesied at this time, became the great treasures of the Jewish people. The Judeans carried with them into exile the laws of their fathers which they inherited from the earliest days of their history and the ideals of justice which they heard again and again from the prophets. Added to these laws was the spirit of kindness and goodness taken from the Book of Deuteronomy. This was not all. They rejected the idea of a God who could be fashioned into an image or who could be seen. The thoughts of Elijah, Amos, and Isaiah came to life as the Judeans went into exile believing in a God of the entire universe, not confined to the boundaries of any one country. This was the distinguishing mark between them and the nations they would encounter in many years to come.

QUESTIONS TO TALK OVER IN CLASS

Which is true: Jeremiah believed that Judah should try to become a strong power with a great army? Jeremiah believed that Judah should be inwardly strong, with its people following the laws of Moses and the religion of their forefathers?

Can you give some examples to prove your point?

What other prophet agreed with Jeremiah?

Jeremiah has been called "the man of sorrows." We might also call him "the man of peace." Give some reasons why both these names are appropriate.

What advice did Jeremiah give the Judeans in Babylonia?

READ

Stories of the Prophets by Landman
    "The Closing Days," pp. 261–279.
The Voice of the Prophets by Gamoran
    Page 63 and the first three lines on page 64.
    "True Glory," p. 78.
Aleph-Bet Story Book by Deborah Pessin
    "Samek and the Cedar Tree," p. 114.

Unit 8

Beginning Again

Have you ever been away from home? How good it looked to you on your return. Imagine then the joy of the Judeans when they learned that they might return from exile to their homeland.

What happened in Babylon during the exile and in Judea after the return carries us through a long stretch of years. The hardships of beginning again were combined with other struggles which threatened the future of Judaism. Leaders came to help and strengthen the people during difficult times. Some of the customs of Jewish life which are observed now began in those days in rebuilt Judea.

With song they return

24. THE CRUCIAL TEST

THE EXILED Judeans came to Babylonia, the land of their conqueror. At first all seemed lost. They were far from home, with memories of a burning Temple and a ruined land. Their king was a captive. Would they share the fate of Israel and disappear from the world?

But Babylonia was not Assyria. It treated its captives very differently, and what might have been the end was only the beginning of a new life. When the Assyrians conquered the Northern Kingdom, the Israelites were scattered over many lands. Families were separated. We can only guess that in the strange lands in which the exiles found themselves, they were too weak or too few in number to continue as a group. Perhaps the cruel conqueror forbade them to practice their religion and to observe their festivals. For the most part the final chapter in the history of Israel was written.

Not so in Babylonia. Nebuchadnezzar had accomplished his purpose. Never again would Jerusalem hold out against him. He was satisfied. Now that the Jews were in Babylonia they were permitted to practice their religion, enjoy their holidays, and live together as a people. Their priests and prophets had come with them and guided them.

Babylonia was a new world to the Judeans. They saw larger

cities, more magnificent buildings and more wealth and luxury than they had ever seen before. Even the land was different. Instead of the rocky Judean hills, there were broad fields
and a system of canals to water them. Food grew easily. Life
in many ways was simpler and more comfortable. The exiles
followed Jeremiah's advice—built homes, tilled fields, and
lived peacefully in the land. In time some Jews rose high in
position and had important posts in the king's household. To
their surprise and joy, they were joined by one group of Israelites who had managed to keep together and at last to steal
away from their Assyrian rulers. After Nebuchadnezzar died,
King Jehoiachin, who had been imprisoned in 597 B.C.E., when
the first exiles came to Babylonia, was freed, and he was given
a high place in the court.

Pleasant homes and goodly fields and high positions are not
the things which stand out in the Babylonian Exile. Other rewards came which had not been dreamed of. Prophets spoke,
poets sang songs of sadness and of hope, history was written
down, and new ways of Jewish living were developed. Something very important was learned. Jews could be away from
their homeland and still remain Jews.

Two prophets are known as the prophets of the exile. Their prophecies are different from those we have read about. No longer were they angry with the people. Now that punishment had come to them, the prophets looked to a better time, and assured the people that God had not forsaken them.

The first of these men was a priest named Ezekiel. He called on the people to have courage and not to despair.

Among the people there were some who complained and said, "Why are we in exile? We are suffering for the wrongdoings of our fathers." For them Ezekiel had a message—a message that opened their eyes to the importance of their own behavior.

Every man, said Ezekiel, is responsible for his own actions. The wicked son of a just father suffers for his own wickedness. However, the righteous son of a wicked man does not suffer for his father's wrong deeds.

Back in Jeremiah's days, the same question was asked. Jeremiah's answer was similar to Ezekiel's. He gave an example that every man could understand. He declared,

> . . . they shall say no more;
> "The fathers have eaten sour grapes
> And the children's teeth are set on edge."

He meant, too, that only those who sinned would be punished.

Have you ever read the poem in which the following lines occur?

> I am the master of my fate,
> I am the captain of my soul.

They were written by a poet not so very long ago. In Rome,

at the time of Julius Caesar, a writer wrote these words, "Every man is the architect of his own soul." Isn't it interesting that Jeremiah and Ezekiel expressed this same idea, which was echoed by other writers so many years later? Ezekiel's listeners realized that it was up to each one of them to make a good life for himself, no matter where he found himself.

Ezekiel also had a message for the exiles as a group. When they lost hope he gathered them together and told them of a vision he had seen. He said that God had shown him a valley of dry bones and asked him, "Can these bones live?" The prophet looked at the dry bones and answered, "O Lord God, Thou knowest." Then God commanded him to prophesy on the dry bones. As Ezekiel prophesied, God put flesh on the bones and breathed life into them and they lived. Then Ezekiel declared that God had said, "These bones are the whole house of Israel. They say, 'Behold, our bones are dried up, our hope is lost, we are clean cut off.'" But God continued and said, "O My people, I will put My spirit in you and ye shall live and I will place you in your own land and ye shall know that I, the Lord, have spoken and performed it."

Can you imagine the effect of such a prophecy and such a promise? Surely, the people thought, the time of return would come.

We know that Ezekiel came with the exiles from Jerusalem and then lived with his people in Babylon. But there is another prophet of the exile about whom we know very little. We do not even know his name. His words are considered the loftiest and the noblest ever uttered by any man. At some time when his writings were being gathered, it was seen that his ideas were like those of the earlier prophet, Isaiah, and so they were added to the prophecies of Isaiah. For that reason he is called the second Isaiah. The writings in the Book of Isaiah beginning with Chapter 40 are believed to be the work of this splendid figure.

Like Ezekiel, he consoled his people.

> Comfort ye, comfort ye, My people,
> Saith your God.
> Bid Jerusalem take heart,
> And proclaim unto her
> That her time of service is accomplished,
> That her guilt is paid off;
> That she hath received of the Lord's hand
> Double for all her sins.

The prophecy ends with these exciting words:

> They that wait for the Lord shall renew their
>   strength;
> They shall mount up with wings as eagles;
> They shall run and not be weary;
> They shall walk and not faint.

The people listened and took heart. The prophet was a keen observer of events. He saw that mighty Babylon was weakening; that from the east an impressive figure was approaching. Cyrus, the new master of the Persian Empire, was soon to conquer Babylonia. The prophet declared that Cyrus "would perform the task which God had given him, to cast down Babylonia and to free the exiles."

Isaiah II's greatest message was still to come. It was a link in the chain which began hundreds of years earlier in the land of Israel, when the stirring words of Amos were uttered. The second Isaiah spoke of a universal God, one who loves and cares for all people, whose "house shall be called a house of prayer for all people," and who declares, "The heaven is My throne and the earth is My footstool."

In one prophecy, Isaiah II told a little story to help the people understand how foolish it was to worship an idol made of wood. He described a man who planted a tree and, when the tree had grown large, he took a part of it to build a fire for himself. He warmed himself at the fire and with its heat he baked bread and roasted meat.

Then the man said, "Aha, I am warm, I have seen the fire." All this was very fine, but the man was not finished using the tree. With the rest of it he fashioned a graven image. Then he fell down and prayed to the image, saying, "Deliver me, for thou art my god." In this way, the prophet poked fun at the man who worshipped an image which he, himself, had made from the trunk of a tree.

However, by now the Jews understood the message of the prophets. From this time forth, the Jewish people never thought or wrote of a national god or a god held in by boundaries of land or sea. Isaiah II's idea of the universal God is an expression of all the pleading, all the thinking, and all the writing about God which had come from the mighty prophets and leaders of the Bible.

As the Jews became accustomed to life in the exile, they found new ways of strengthening their religious life. Without the Temple, there could be no sacrifices, but they could get together to hear the Levites sing, to hear someone read from the books of history, and to pray together with the priests. The priests brought with them the scrolls of the Torah, so that it was not forgotten. At some time during this period some of the historical books of the Bible began to be written. It is possible that parts of the books of Judges, Samuel, and Kings were read aloud to the people as they gathered together on the Sabbath. We can be sure that such gatherings would unite them and help them remember what happened in days gone by. Years later, when the Jews were scattered over all the world, prayer, songs, and the reading of the Torah took the place of sacrifices. This new way of worship had its beginnings in the Babylonian Exile.

At last the almost unbelievable occurred. The kingdom of Babylonia fell to the new world power, Persia, led by the great Cyrus. Babylon, the capital city, surrendered without a struggle. Cyrus was now master of a tremendous empire, including all the lands that had once belonged both to Assyria and to Babylonia. He was a wise conqueror. He knew it would strengthen his rule to have a loyal state between his land and Egypt. In addition, he could afford to be generous and he was. In 538 B.C.E. a royal proclamation was read to the Jews:

Thus saith Cyrus king of Persia: All the Kingdoms of the Earth hath the Lord, the God of Heaven, given me; and He hath charged me to build Him a house in Jerusalem, which is in Judah. Whosoever there is among you of all His people—let him go up to Jerusalem, and build the house of the Lord, the God of Israel. . . . And whosoever is left, in any place where he sojourneth, let the men of his place help him with the silver, and with gold, and with goods, and with beasts, beside the free-will offering for the house of God which is in Jerusalem.

The exile was ended. The road to Jerusalem was open.

QUESTIONS TO ANSWER IN CLASS

What lesson for the future did the Jews learn from the Babylonian Exile?

Who were the two great prophets of the exile?

What new world power conquered Babylonia? What king ended the exile?

SOMETHING TO DO

Write a composition comparing the way the Assyrians treated the Israelites and the way the Babylonians treated the Judeans. What were the results of the two exiles?

Explain in your own words: "I am the architect of my own soul."

Find out about the Balfour Declaration. How does it compare with the Proclamation of Cyrus?

READ

The Voice of the Prophets by Gamoran
   "The New Covenant," p. 99,
   "A Proverb Explained," p. 111.
Compare these two prophecies:
   "Comfort Ye, My People," p. 23,
   "The Valley of Dry Bones," p. 120.
The New Jewish History, Book III, by Mamie G. Gamoran, pp. 259–261, 273.
Lost Worlds by White
   "Mistress of Kingdoms," pp. 219–228.

READINGS FOR TEACHERS

Unit VIII (*CHAPTERS 24–26*)

The Bible, Ezra; Neh. 1, 2, 4:9–6, 8, 10:29–11, 12:27–12:47, 13.
The Jews, Chap. I, pp. 48–55.
A History of the Jewish People by Margolis and Marx, Chaps. XXII, XXIII.
   or
A History of the Jews by Solomon Grayzel, Chaps. I, II.
Preface to Scripture by Freehof, Part Two, Chap. V, pp. 114–120, 131–143; Chap. VI, pp. 184–196.
Israel in the Ancient Near East by Orlinsky, Chap. VII.

25. REBUILDING THE LAND

When the Lord brought back those that returned to Zion,
We were like unto them that dream.
Then was our mouth filled with laughter,
And our tongue with singing;
Then said they among the nations:
"The Lord hath done great things with these."
The Lord hath done great things with us;
We are rejoiced.

History, you see, can be told in many ways. Even the poet is sometimes a historian. The man who wrote this psalm was telling how his people were returning to their native soil after a long exile and helping us to understand the joy and delight which they felt at the opportunity to come back to Jerusalem. We can also see how religious faith would be strengthened, as they realized that the great prophecies of return were coming true.

According to the Bible, 42,360 Jews made the trip back to Judea from Babylonia. Some Jews who remained behind sent gifts and money to Jerusalem for the work of rebuilding that lay ahead.

Judea was a very small country with only one important city, Jerusalem, and some surrounding territory. Those Jews who had remained were the poorest of all. They had been left in a land ruined by war. They were still poor and weak. All around, the ancient enemies of the country moved in and settled down. Edom and Moab were to the south and the east, and to the north lived the Samaritans.

The pilgrims returned with two leaders, Zerubbabel, the grandson of King Jehoiachin, who was a direct descendant of David, and Joshua, a priest who came from a long line of priestly ancestors. The first years were filled with work. Houses had to be built and farms laid out. Fields which had lain fallow for years had to be turned over and sowed. Vineyards were replanted and terraces replaced on Judean hills. It was not easy. The rains did not come. Crops failed. People lost their courage and their hope.

The Temple was to be rebuilt. In spite of all, no one forgot the task which Cyrus charged the Judeans to carry out. For this purpose he gave back many of the sacred vessels and objects which Nebuchadnezzar had captured and had taken to Babylonia. Before long the foundation was laid. An altar

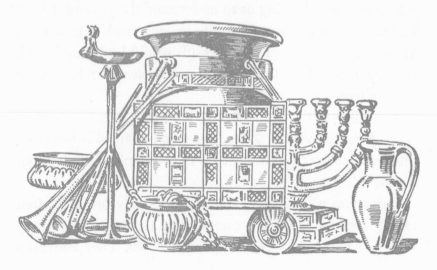

was built in the court of the First Temple, and there the people worshipped.

The most determined enemies of the new colonists were the Samaritans. They did their best to hinder the rebuilding of the Temple. From their name you can guess that they lived in Samaria and you remember that this had been the capital of Israel. When the Israelites were driven out, Assyria sent into the land other captives from other lands. They lived together with those Israelites who had managed to escape the Assyrian soldiers and developed a religion which was a mixture of their old worship and that of the Israelites.

When the newcomers first returned to Jerusalem, the Samaritans sent them a message. They wanted to help in rebuilding the Temple. The Jews had to decide what to do. What would happen if the Samaritans shared the work of rebuilding the Temple? They would then come to worship in it. They might want to bring some of their ideas into the prayers, perhaps even images into the holy building. The Jews refused the offer. From that time on the Samaritans became their bitter enemies. Whenever it seemed that an effort would be made to build, the Samaritans tried to stop it. They had all sorts of tricks. They wrote letters to the king in Persia saying that the Jews were about to set up an independent kingdom. Back came the king's messenger with the order, "Stop building!"

For nine years nothing could be done. Would all the hope and plans come to naught? Once again there were prophets who urged the people to action. The prophet Haggai spoke to Zerubbabel and to Joshua, "Thus saith the Lord of hosts: Consider your ways. Go up to the hill-country and bring

wood, and build the house, and I will take pleasure in it." He
promised them that the Temple would be even more beautiful than before, when he said, "Thus saith the Lord of hosts:
Yet once, it is a little while, and I will shake the heavens and
the earth and the sea, and the dry land; and I will shake all
nations, and the choicest things of all nations shall come, and
I will fill this house with glory. The glory of this latter house
shall be greater than that of the former, and in this place will
I give peace."

Another prophet named Zechariah encouraged the people.
Letters went again to the new king, Darius. They pleaded
with him to search for the orders which Cyrus had given.
When Darius found the proclamation, he saw that the Jews
were right. He wanted to see the work completed. He sent
his permission. With this encouragement everyone went to
work with a will. At last the Temple was finished in 516 B.C.E.

Do you remember Jeremiah's promise that the exile would
last only seventy years? From 586 B.C.E., the year when the
First Temple was destroyed, to 516 B.C.E., the year when the
Second Temple was built, is exactly seventy years!

The Psalms tell us again of the joy with which the great
event was hailed. There are many psalms of thanksgiving and
praise which were written and sung at about this time. One
of these is Psalm 85 which begins:

> Lord, Thou hast been favourable unto Thy land,
> Thou hast brought back the captivity of Jacob.
> Thou hast forgiven the iniquity of Thy people,
> Thou hast pardoned all their sin. Selah.

It ends:

Yea, the Lord will give that which is good;
And our land shall yield her produce.
Righteousness shall go before Him,
And shall set us in the way of His steps.

This Temple was not as large or as beautiful as Solomon's Temple had been. There was still much to be done to beautify it. That did not matter. By building the Temple the colonists proved that they had determination and courage and the will to carry out what they started to do.

In Babylon the Jews waited eagerly for news from Judea. How did the Jews fare there? They must have rejoiced when they heard that the Temple had at last been erected. Then came other news. Zerubbabel was no longer at the head of the country. A Persian governor sent by Darius and then by the new ruler, Xerxes, collected taxes and took care of military matters. As far as the people were concerned, their ruler was the High Priest. He had charge of religious matters and was recognized by the king. This was the beginning of a new form of government for the Jewish people. For many years

to come the country would be ruled by a High Priest who took his authority from the Persian king. This kind of government, under a religious leader, is called a theocracy.

For many years, the word from Judea was not good. Taxes were heavy, the land was poor. Hebrew was not the only language spoken. A new language, Aramaic, had come in and was crowding out Hebrew in ordinary conversation. The religious life of the Jews needed help. Many Jews had taken wives from among the nations which surrounded the country. Strange religious customs had crept into the Temple worship. Something had to be done.

There are two books in the Bible which tell what happened at this time. They are called Ezra and Nehemiah, and are named after two men. Both of them did very interesting and exciting things.

While things in Judea were in a sorry state, in Babylonia there was a strong Jewish community. The Jews who had remained there were well treated and lived comfortably. They were traders, farmers, and craftsmen. Some had high positions in the king's court. They had continued to follow their religion, to study the Torah, and to teach their children. The people gathered to hear the priests speak on the Sabbaths. No doubt that was when they asked, "How fare our brethren in Jerusalem?"

When the stories that all was not well in Judea came to Babylon, a priest named Ezra decided that he would go to see for himself what was happening. He was a scribe, a learned teacher of the Torah, a descendant of a long line of priests. He gathered a large band of followers, more than 1,600 people, and received the king's permission to go to Ju-

dea. From all sides he received gifts and money to take along to Jerusalem. Even the king gave Ezra fine gifts for the Temple.

The six-hundred-mile journey led over river, desert and mountain. Ezra and his followers arrived in Jerusalem. What did they find?

The Jews received Ezra with great honor. They no longer had such learned men in their midst. But their honor did not give Ezra much joy. He saw that the rumors which had reached Babylon were indeed true. A great many of the Jews, even priests, had taken foreign wives. They were Canaanites, Moabites, Ammonites and Egyptians, and they brought with them many of their religious customs. The laws in the Torah were not being followed. The Sabbath was not being kept. The rich oppressed the poor and justice was not found in the land.

The Jews assembled to listen to Ezra. When they saw how shocked he was at what he had found in his visit, and how he wept as he prayed, they were ashamed. They made a promise to send all the foreign wives home. One by one the men rose to make this vow.

Not everyone agreed with Ezra. A whole book was written against this decision. It showed how good and kind a woman from another people could be. This was the Book of Ruth, which is in the Bible.

The story of Ruth tells of a young woman from Moab, who came to live in the town of Bethlehem in Canaan, at the time of the Judges. She took care of her mother-in-law, Naomi, and was kind to her. The story relates how later on Ruth married Boaz, a farmer of Bethlehem. There is more to the Book of Ruth than just a beautiful story. It tries to teach a lesson. For it tells that the son of Ruth and Boaz was the grandfather of David, the beloved king. The beautiful and kind woman from Moab was the ancestor of the great rulers of Judah.

You can see how the Bible gives both sides of the serious problem which faced the Judeans. On the one hand, Ezra felt that foreign wives had to leave the land in order to keep different ideas of worship and living out of Judea. On the other hand, the unknown author of the Book of Ruth told that the royal family of Judah came from Ruth, the Moabitess.

The Judeans followed Ezra's advice. It was not easy to carry out their promise to send away their foreign wives. When the women went home, their families became angry. Jerusalem was attacked. Other troubles began. Ezra decided it was necessary to strengthen the walls of the city. Quickly enemies sent word to the king—the Jews are building a wall. They will break away from Persia. The work was stopped. Ezra, the priest, could do no more. Another and a stronger hand was needed.

Again help came from Babylon. One of the king's most im-

portant nobles, his cupbearer, named Nehemiah, was a Jew.
He heard the bad news. He begged for permission to go to
Judea. The king appointed him governor and sent him off.
Nehemiah came with only a small group. He did not let anyone know of his coming. He wanted to see for himself just
what was going on. For three days he went about the city of
Jerusalem, just as though he were an ordinary visitor. In the
dead of night, when no one was watching, he walked around
the city walls. Quietly he learned what he wanted to know.

Nehemiah was a man of action. He made his plans. He
called the men of the city together and announced that the
king had sent him to be governor of the land. He did not
waste a moment. Work started immediately on the city walls,
broken and fallen down. All the men were called to labor.
They knew that their enemies would soon be upon them. With
one hand, says the Book of Nehemiah, they worked. With
the other, they held a weapon, ready for action. Nehemiah
rode around with a horn, ready to sound it at the first sign of
danger.

Nehemiah put a new heart into the people. They worked hard. The walls of the city were rebuilt. For the first time in many years, everyone felt safe.

This was only the beginning, Nehemiah's keen eyes had seen more than the crumbling city walls. He saw, as Ezra had seen, that the Torah was being forgotten. The city gates were open on the Sabbath for trading. No one watched out for the poor of the land. After bad seasons, poor farmers lost their land. Some of them sold their children as slaves to pay their debts.

Nehemiah called the wealthy men of the city together. He begged them to change their ways. He did more than talk. He was a wealthy man himself. People owed him money, too. He set everyone an example. He forgave all those who owed him money. He did not take the taxes that were due him as a governor. Because there had been a drought, he gave grain to those who needed it. Nehemiah's good example was followed. Clothes and land were returned and debtors and Jewish slaves were freed.

Now, Nehemiah called on Ezra who seems to have been

forgotten these many years. Together they prepared a set of laws, following the commandments of the Books of Moses. For the first time in many years, the people built tabernacles and celebrated the holiday of Sukos. They agreed to keep the laws concerning the Sabbath and the holidays, and not to marry men and women from other groups. They promised to protect the poor and to judge all people honestly.

After some years there was a final split between Samaritans and Jews. The Samaritans built their own temple on Mt. Gerizim. They kept to themselves. They did not marry with other groups. Today, in Israel, after all these years, you will still find a few descendants of this ancient people in Jerusalem and in Nablus on the West Bank, practicing their religion in the ancient way.

Nehemiah, with Ezra's help, strengthened the land, the law, and the people. His honesty, his courage, and his ability helped the Jews at a time when their future hung in the balance. In the years following his work in Judea, the little land began a period of peaceful activity. The people were united. The hardships of beginning again were overcome. The Jews were established once more in their homeland.

QUESTIONS TO TALK OVER IN CLASS

What hardships faced the returning Judeans?
Who helped them overcome their difficulties?
How would you describe Ezra?
How would you describe Nehemiah?
What made them a good team?
Which neighbors made trouble for the newcomers?
Does a writer of history use only books to learn what happened long ago? What else gives him information? Can you give some examples from this book?

WORK FOR A COMMITTEE

Prepare a little play for your class, telling the story of Ruth. Here are some suggestions to help you plan it. Have a Narrator give an introduction and tell when this story happened. Follow with:

Scene 1. The parting of Naomi and Orpah. Give Ruth's words, "Entreat me not to leave thee."

Scene 2. The meeting of Ruth and Boaz. Tell how Boaz gave Ruth permission to glean in his fields.

Close the play by having the Narrator tell about Ruth's son and his descendants.

READ

Universal Jewish Encyclopedia, Vol. IX.

Look up the article about the Samaritans. There are some interesting pictures on pages 334–337.

The Unconquered by Gaer
   "Cup-Bearer to the King," p. 43.
With Singer and Sage by Gamoran
   "Ruth," p. 227.

26. THE QUIET YEARS

THERE are times in a person's life when nothing special seems to happen. Boys and girls go to school, year after year, then come the times of Bar Mitzvah and Confirmation, and suddenly without anyone's seeming to realize it, they are grown up, going to high school and thinking about college.

In the same way there are periods in the life of a people during which nothing special seems to happen. Yet, at the end of this period of one or two centuries, many changes have taken place. The nation may have become strong or weak, its people may have learned better ways of living, and the years of peace may have brought unity to the land.

The little land of Judea now entered upon such a quiet period. We do not know exactly what happened during the next hundred years. From the few records which have come down to us, we have formed a general idea of the kind of life which was followed in Judea during this time. It was ruled by the High Priest. He was both the civil and religious ruler. His civil authority came from the Persian king. Most of the rulers of Persia were just and generous. Their domain stretched far and wide. They made only a few demands on their territories. The Judeans were supposed to pay their taxes and to send some of their young men for the Persian army.

On the whole, Judea was left alone to take care of its own affairs. The religious authority of the High Priest came from the Five Books of Moses. All the laws of his office were found in the Torah.

The last of the great Hebrew prophets appeared in the early days of this period, probably shortly after Nehemiah's time. He was known as Malachi, which means "my messenger." Malachi's words added force to the work of Ezra and Nehemiah. He spoke to the priests who neglected their duty and reminded them of their important position:

> For the priest's lips should keep knowledge,
> And they (the people) should seek the law at his mouth;
> For he is the messenger of the Lord of hosts.

Then he turned to the men who were acting unjustly and said:

> I will be a swift witness . . .
> Against those that oppress the hireling in his wages,
> The widow, and the fatherless,
> And that turn aside the stranger from his right . . .
> Saith the Lord of hosts.

Although Malachi scolded the Jews, he also reminded them of God's love for all men. One of the most famous passages in the Book of Malachi begins with the words:

> Have we not all one father?
> Hath not one God created us?

Malachi's words brought to a fitting close the wonderful books of prophecy in the Bible.

Judea, at this time, was a country of farmers, shepherds, and craftsmen. Jerusalem, the only large city, was not a center of commerce. It was a religious center. Here the High Priest with his assistant priests lived. In the Temple they followed out the laws of sacrifice and worship which were laid down in the Five Books of Moses. The Torah was the law of the land and was faithfully carried out. On market days, the judges sat and judged, and the people would congregate and hear the Torah being read.

The High Priest had power and wealth. He had the privilege of taxing the people. Together with the other priests, he received a portion of the best of the crops and the animals from the people when they brought sacrifices to the Temple. The Levites, who assisted in the Temple, and the priests who went out into the villages to teach and pray received a regular portion of the crops. Gradually, power and riches passed into the hands of two classes—the priests and the large land owners.

The small farmers, shepherds, and artisans lived quietly in their little homes. There was enough for their families and enough left over to pay the "t'rumo," which means the portion belonging to the priests. They cultivated their small holdings, taught their children the prayers, songs, and laws of their people, and were satisfied with the life they lived.

A new group of leaders began to appear. They were called scribes. Some were priests like Ezra; others were merely learned men who knew the Torah well. Originally, the scribes acted as secretaries, with a title like "Keeper of the King's Records." Since they were among the few who could read and write, they copied down other things of value, like the words of the prophets, the Scrolls of the Law, or the stories of their people.

You remember when the scroll of Deuteronomy was found. It was first brought to Shafan, a scribe, who took it to the king and read it to him. When the Jews went into exile, the scribes, together with the priests, carried with them their treasures, not of gold and silver, but of precious scrolls and undying wisdom, and made sure they were not forgotten.

The scribes grew more important when the Jews returned from exile. New customs and ceremonies developed. Schools opened, and the scribes taught the children. Adults learned

history, law, and wisdom when they heard the Torah and portions from the prophets read on Sabbaths and festivals.

At some time during these years the Bible, as we know it now, began to take shape. Certain books were considered precious and were set aside from all the other books. This was called putting them in the canon. "Canon" is a Greek word which means a rod, or a carpenter's rule. Thus these books were measured or examined to decide if they were worthy of being considered holy, different from all other books. The word, canon, came into use many years later. However, it was during Ezra's day, and the years that followed, that certain books began to be accepted as sacred. These chosen books became the Bible. Strangely enough, the word Bible is also a Greek word. Originally it meant paper and then book. Today, of course, the Bible means only one Book, the great collection of Hebrew laws, ideals, and literature, known as the Book of Books.

The Bible is divided into three parts, the Torah, or the Five Books of Moses, the Prophets, and the Writings.

From very ancient times the Five Books of Moses were considered holy because people believed that they were written at the command of God. We can learn something from the Samaritans, whose customs were so very like the customs of the Jews. Their holy books consist only of the Torah and part of the Book of Joshua. We believe that these are the books which were counted holy before the Judeans went into exile, for that is when the Samaritans appear in Jewish history.

After the days of the Babylonian Exile, the other early historical books like Joshua and Judges became part of the sacred literature. The scribes usually copied these scrolls on papyrus

or on leather. A copy of the Torah written by a scribe became a precious possession.

A book which appears much later says that Nehemiah founded a library and gathered together the "acts of the kings and the prophets, and of David." This would make us believe that Nehemiah might have begun setting aside some of the books of the second part of the Bible. This part is called Prophets. It consists of the books of Joshua, Judges, Samuel, and Kings, and the fifteen books of the literary prophets from Isaiah to Malachi.

For many years there were discussions by the rabbis and learned men about the other books which finally came into the third part of the Bible, called the Writings. It was not until about 200 c.e. that thirty-nine books which make up the Bible were all accepted as the Holy Scriptures. A number of other scrolls which were considered and discussed had not been found excellent enough to go into the Bible. These were gathered in a book called the Apocrypha, which means hidden, and contains many interesting books of wisdom and history. The whole story of the Maccabean revolt and victory which you will learn soon is found in the Apocrypha. In the Catholic church, the Apocrypha is considered a part of the Bible.

The priests and scribes of Judea were building foundations for the future. They began some customs which became part of Jewish life for centuries to come. In the Temple in Jerusalem, and even in the little villages and towns, there were gatherings for daily prayers. The singing of psalms at worship began at this time. Some of the laws of the Torah were not clear, and teachers and scribes began to interpret and explain how they applied to the every-day life of the people. These interpretations of the Law were called the Midrash, and in time they became very important.

Although the priests had great power, sometimes they called on the people. They had an advisory council which helped them rule. This was made up mainly of large land owners and farmers. Sometimes, ordinary men from all over the country came together to decide certain important questions. This larger group was called the Anshei K'neses Hag'dolo, or Great Assembly. The Great Assembly was not a body which met regularly, like the Congress of the United States. It came together only to discuss a special question upon which the leaders in the advisory council could not agree. After a decision was made the members of the Great Assembly would go home. From these meetings we learn that the leaders did not take all the power to themselves. The plain people also took part in making important decisions.

Commerce and trading with the outside world were not very great, but letters and messengers came from Jewish communities outside of Judea. In Babylon, there were thousands of Jews, many of them rich and important, and Jews lived in other parts of Persia, too. When you celebrate Purim and read about the Book of Esther, you learn about the life of some Jews in Persia. In Egypt, a colony of Israelites and Judeans had flourished for over 200 years. A brand new city, Alexandria, was being settled, and Jews would soon play an important part in the life there.

The Jews in Judea, living quietly in their small country, took little part in the busy, bustling life of the great countries which surrounded them. They did not know that these quiet years would be followed by a tremendous struggle which would determine whether they were to live or die as a people. The quiet years were not wasted years. During this time the Jews became a unified group. Their children grew up in peace, loving their land, learning the Torah and honoring the traditions that had come to them from their earliest ancestors. All this would stand them in good stead in the years to come.

QUESTIONS TO TALK OVER IN CLASS

In what way did the men of Judea share in governing their country? What was the name for the kind of religious government they lived under? What is the name for the kind of government in our country?

In what countries were Jews living at this time?

What are some of the things you have learned about the Bible in this chapter?

SOMETHING TO DO

Arrange in the correct time order these leaders: Judges, Patriarchs, Lawgivers, Kings, Scribes, Prophets, Priests.

Name one man or woman from each group.

Pick out five quotations from the Bible which you read in this book that were new to you. From which books of the Bible were they taken? Memorize two that you like the best.

Unit 9

The Brave Maccabees

A clash of ideas, followed by a clash of arms is found in the last unit in our book. Twice before, the people who began with Abraham might have been lost. One branch, the kingdom of Israel, disappeared, but Judah lived even through exile. This time danger faced them from two sides. The first was a threat to their religion and the ways of living which they had developed in their land. The second was danger of conquest at the hands of a mighty army.

The Maccabean heroes decided the issue.

Who is for the Lord, follow me!

27. THE WORLD COMES IN

FOR TWO hundred years the kings of Persia controlled a vast empire. Suddenly from the west came a new conqueror who, like Cyrus, Nebuchadnezzar, and the kings of Assyria, each in turn, swept away all the armies which faced him and became the ruler of the entire Mediterranean world. The name of this young warrior was Alexander and he is known in history as Alexander the Great. From Greece into Asia, down the coast of Syria and Judea, and into Egypt marched Alexander with his forces, and all the countries fell before him. Then at last he entered Persia where he took the capital city of Susa and the mighty Babylon. Alexander became master of a greater territory than any man before him. All this happened in thirteen years, between the years of 334 and 321 B.C.E.

Judea was only a small spot in Alexander's world. He entered Jerusalem and took the city with his soldiers. The Jews did not resist him. Instead of paying tribute to Darius of Persia, they began to send their taxes to Alexander. They hoped their life in their own country would continue as before. They did not want to become part of the world outside, the great glittering Greek Empire.

Alexander was a pupil of one of the greatest Greek teachers.

He believed that Greek ideas and customs were the best and the most wonderful in the world. Wherever he went he wanted to spread Greek learning and Greek ways of living. After he conquered a land he settled some of his soldiers in its cities. They brought Greek customs into their new homes. Greek became the language of the land. The soldiers built temples for the worship of Greek gods and goddesses, and gymnasiums for the athletic sports and contests they loved.

Judea did not attract many Greek soldiers at first. It was a small land and did not offer promise of wealth or an easy life. The other countries in Alexander's realm accepted Greek ideas. Syria to the north and Egypt to the south were centers of Greek life. Judea was surrounded by a Greek world.

Alexander died suddenly after a reign of only thirteen years. Then there was chaos. Alexander left no heir. Who would reign in his place?

For many years his generals fought among themselves. Finally his kingdom was divided. The southern part was held by a general named Ptolemy, who declared himself king of Egypt. He reigned in Alexandria, the new and beautiful city which Alexander had built along the Mediterranean, on the coast of Egypt. The large northern portion of Alexander's realm was held by the Syrians. Their ruler was a general named Seleucus, who reigned in the new city of Antioch, on the coast of Syria. Seleucus was not happy that Ptolemy controlled so much territory. Every now and then he would march down the coast of the Mediterranean Sea to attack Egypt. Battles were fought on the soil of Judea. It was caught, as so often before, at the crossroads between two great powers of the world.

For over a hundred years Judea was in the possession of the Ptolemies of Egypt. These Egyptian kings were, on the whole, kind rulers. At first they did not interfere with Judea. The High Priest continued to conduct the affairs of the country and to collect the taxes. Part of them remained with the High Priest for the Temple and the needs of the land, and a share went to the king in Alexandria.

Then the king made an important change. He issued an order from Alexandria. The High Priest, called Simon the Just, a good and righteous man, lost his power to collect the taxes. The king appointed Simon's grandson, Joseph, who was his friend, to collect the taxes. For this privilege Joseph paid the king a large sum of money. Then he went out to collect much more from the people. He sent tax collectors throughout the land. The taxes which did not go to the king were kept by Joseph for his own use. He became very wealthy. He appointed his friends to high positions.

Judea was no longer a land separated from the great world outside. Officials of the king, like Joseph, and merchants who had business in the great seaport of Alexandria and other cities often traveled down to Egypt. Once a large band of scholars was invited to come to Alexandria for an important purpose. This is how it happened.

By this time many Jews lived in Egypt, especially in Alexandria. They took part in the busy life of the city. Some families had left Judea many years before and they no longer spoke or read Hebrew. They knew only Greek. They followed Greek fashions and read Greek books. However, they did not forget that they were Jews. They did not follow the Greek religion. They wanted to read the Bible. They wished their

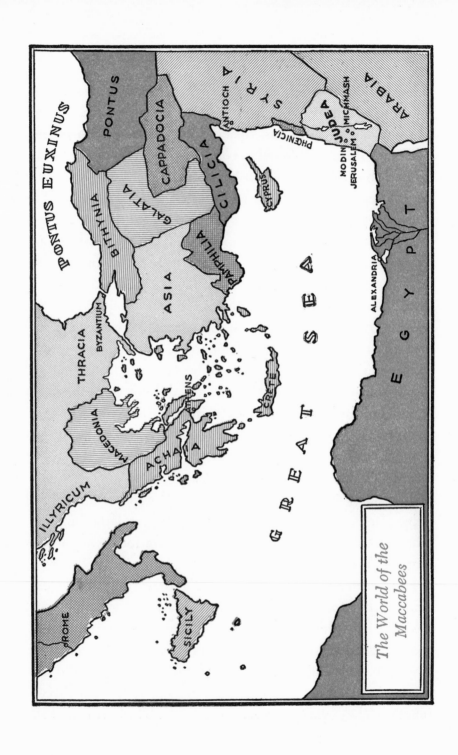

The World of the Maccabees

children to know the history of their people and to read the noble words of the prophets. They were eager to have the people in whose midst they lived learn about their literature and to become acquainted with its wisdom and beauty. For their sake the Bible was translated into Greek. Seventy-two scholars were invited by the king of Egypt to come to Alexandria to translate the Five Books of Moses into Greek.

There is a legend that when the scholars arrived in Alexandria, each was conducted to a small room where he worked alone until he had finished his translation. In seventy-two days each of the scholars had completed his work. The story says that to everyone's amazement each translation was exactly alike! This was the first translation of the Bible into a foreign tongue. The Greek translation is called the Septuagint, meaning seventy, in honor of the scholars. (No doubt the word seventy-two would not have made a good name.) The exact date of the Septuagint is unknown. It probably appeared at about 250 B.C.E.

In 197 B.C.E., after much fighting between Egypt and Syria, Judea passed from the hands of the Egyptians and came under the rule of Syria. The Syrian king ruled from Antioch. He stationed Syrian soldiers in Judean cities. Jews in high offices now looked to Antioch for favors.

During the years under Egyptian rule and especially under the Syrians, Greek influences began to be felt in Judea. Jews were traveling back and forth to Alexandria, to Antioch, and to other foreign cities. They saw different customs being followed and different ways of living. How simple the city of Jerusalem must have looked to travelers who returned from their journeys! Some Jews became dissatisfied. They longed for changes. They began to imitate everything Greek. In Jerusalem many young Jews wore Greek clothes, spoke Greek, went to Greek schools, and changed their names from Hebrew to Greek. Joshua became Jason. Alexander and Menelaus became favorite names. Sports and games became popular. Young priests left their duties and studies in the Temple to take part in them.

Wearing a Greek hat or speaking Greek was not the important change. What really mattered was that these Jews were ready to give up their own Jewish teachings and to follow new ideas which were very different from the ones their people had developed. The life of the Jews and the ideas which guided them were almost the exact opposite of Greek ideas and ways of living. What were these differences?

The first way in which these two peoples were unlike was in their religions. The Greek religion was a religion of many gods who lived in the heavens, in the same way that human beings lived on earth. The Greeks wrote stories and poems about them which told how they loved and hated, were sad and happy, and sometimes even behaved badly and were cruel. In these stories the gods did not set an example for human beings to follow. Jews, on the other hand, believed in a God who was better and nobler than any human being. Because of their faith in Him they tried to improve themselves and lead better lives. The teachings of the Prophets, of Deuteronomy, and of the other early books of the Bible, that God wants men to act justly to each other, were foreign to the Greeks. Only a few of their teachers seem to have caught a glimpse of this thought.

Statues of the Greek gods were found in temples and in public buildings. You know how Jews have always been opposed to making statues to represent God, the invisible ruler of the universe. Even the Temple in Jerusalem could not compare with the ornate and stately Greek temples.

The Greek teachers and thinkers studied mathematics and medicine and tried to learn the secrets of the world they lived in. In astronomy, the study of the stars and the heavens, they made important discoveries. Some of their calculations are still used in our own day. An educated person today must know what the Greek thinkers believed, even though he may not agree with their teachings. While the teachers taught young men art and science and mathematics, good deeds were not emphasized. Athletics, sports, and games were an important part of Greek life. Sports arenas and gymnasiums were built in every city and people spent a great deal of time there in play and practice. Thousands of slaves had been captured and brought into Greece and these men and women worked for their Greek masters. Study and games were only for the lucky ones who were born free and rich. Others did not count in the Greek way of life.

Here again you can see many contrasts between the ideas and customs of Jews and Greeks. Jewish scholars studied the Torah and tried to make its laws part of the life of the country. Slavery had little place in Judea at this time. Such pastimes as sports and athletic contests were very strange to Jews.

Not everyone in Judea was satisfied to see the new customs becoming so popular. The country was split into two groups. On the one side were the men and women who were called Hellenists, followers of Greek ways. They were ready to set aside the rules of the Torah and to follow the easy, pleasure-laden Greek customs. The Hellenists were found among the most important people in Jerusalem, those who had connections in Alexandria and in Antioch, and among some of the priestly families of wealth and distinction.

Those who actively resisted the new Greek ways were called the Chasidim, the pious ones. The people, as a whole, followed them. They were loyal to their own customs and commandments. They were determined to keep the laws of the Sabbath, sacrifice, and food which the Jews had followed since Ezra's time. The teachings of the prophets had become part of their life. They would not exchange their ideas of righteousness for beautiful buildings, lovely statues, and ways of living which were unfair to the poor and the downtrodden. Idols and idol-worship had completely vanished from Jewish homes; they could not come back now. The God of Moses, Amos, and Isaiah, who could not be seen or pictured, was their God.

When Judea came under Syrian rule, the king began to interfere directly with the affairs of the country. The Hellenists sought power from their new ruler. They offered gifts and money in return for high positions. There were quarrels among the priests. First one and then another became High Priest. The Syrian king took over the power to appoint the High Priest. In return for a huge bribe he selected one of the Hellenists, named Menelaus, for the high office. Menelaus was disloyal to his people and to his religion. He allowed the king to come into the Temple and to enter the Holy of Holies, that sacred place which the High Priest himself was supposed to enter only once a year. He permitted the king to worship Greek gods on the Temple shrines and to take away with him the holy vessels which were used in the service.

The Chasidim grew angry to see their Temple spoiled and the laws of the Torah mocked at and insulted. Their temper was rising. What of the future? Would the people of Judea follow Hellenism, the Greek way of life, or would they hold fast to Judaism and the Jewish tradition?

QUESTIONS TO ANSWER IN CLASS

What countries divided Alexander's lands between them?
What happened to Judea?
What were some of the differences between the Jewish and the Greek way of life?
How can a country's geography have an effect on its history? Can you give examples from the history of Israel and Judea, and also from modern countries?

READ

The Unconquered by Gaer
"Seventy-two Scribes," p. 89,
"A Knave's End," p. 157.
The Great March by Rose G. Lurie
"With Peace They Conquer," p. 10.

READINGS FOR TEACHERS

Unit IX (*CHAPTERS 27–29*)

A History of the Jewish People by Margolis and Marx, Chaps. XXIV, XXV, XXVI.
or
A History of the Jews by Grayzel, Chaps. III, IV.
Apocrypha, Maccabees I, 1–4.

28. REBELLION

THE CHASIDIM had their backs to the wall. What could they do when the most important man in the country, the High Priest, encouraged the Syrian king to mock their religion?

The new ruler of Judea was named Antiochus IV. His full name was Antiochus Epiphanes, which means the Sacred One. Some people made fun of his name and called him Antiochus Epimanes, the Madman. For some of his actions he deserved this name. During his youth he had been held in Rome as a royal prisoner. In those years he may have planned what he might do if he became master of Syria, or perhaps like Alexander, master of the world. He would make all his territories into Greek countries, speaking Greek, following Greek customs, and worshipping Greek gods. His chance came at last. He became king of Syria.

Before long he went into battle against Egypt. He could not conquer his old enemy and he had to return home defeated. He passed by Jerusalem on his way back to Antioch, capital of Syria. Here he felt he was master and he decided to make the most of his position.

Antiochus was different from the Egyptian kings who had ruled Judea. They did not try to change Jewish religious practices. Antiochus was not satisfied that only one group among the Jews was ready to follow Greek customs. He determined to wipe out Judaism and to force the Jews to accept the Greek religion. He was sure that then all other Greek ideas and customs would sweep through the country.

While Syrian soldiers protected the High Priest, Menelaus, and his followers, other soldiers fell on the Jews. It was a Sabbath. The Chasidim would not fight on the sacred day. Thousands of people were killed. The Chasidim fled to caves, to the mountains outside of Jerusalem, and to the hills of Ephraim. The Temple was ruined. On one terrible day in Kislev, in the year 168 B.C.E., forbidden animals were sacrificed on the altars. The Greek party was in control. The scattered Chasidim were lost unless they found a leader.

Messengers went all over the land with the king's decrees. In every tiny village and hamlet a statue to a Greek god was to be erected. The Jewish religion was forbidden. The scrolls of the Torah were to be destroyed. Those who resisted would be killed. Jews who had lived peacefully in their little villages for centuries saw the hateful signs of the tyrant all around.

At about this time a new book appeared. Later it became part of the Bible. It was the Book of Daniel. It told the miraculous story of Daniel, who was one of the captives led to Babylonia by Nebuchadnezzar. There, with three companions, Daniel was ordered to bow down to idols, to eat forbidden food, to do the very things which the Jews were ordered to do by Antiochus. Daniel refused and was thrown into a den of lions. The fierce beasts did not destroy him. He was saved from the lions because of his faith in God and his devotion to his religion.

The rest of the Book of Daniel is full of tales which have a hidden meaning. They are meant to show how the nations of the world which worshipped idols and men instead of one God were all destroyed. This book brought a message of hope to the Jews who were suffering just as Daniel had suffered. Somehow, they too would be saved.

Another wonderful chapter in the history of our people followed. This is the story of the Maccabees. Every Jewish boy and girl is proud of these few brave men who fought for their religion, their land, and their people.

One quiet morning a band of Syrian soldiers entered the little village of Modin in the Judean hills and gathered the people around. No one knew that what happened there that day would decide the fate of the Jewish people. The Syrians came boldly to show the Jews the new laws in action. A swine would be sacrificed on the altar, not by a Greek, but by a Jew.

Mattathias, an old priest, stood silently watching with the villagers. Although he was eighty years old, his heart was

young and fiery. All were silent. Then came the terrible moment. A Jew stepped to the altar to make the sacrifice. Mattathias raised his arm. The traitor lay dead at the shrine. "Who
is for the Lord?" the ringing voice of Mattathias called out.

Mattathias' five sons stood by their father. The Syrian soldiers were killed or fled in terror as the villagers turned on
them. The fight for freedom had begun.

John, Simon, Judah, Eleazar, and Jonathan were the five
sons of the old priest. With just a few followers they found a
place in the mountains to set up a small camp. At first they
could only lie in ambush and wait to attack small groups of
Syrian soldiers. They knew the country well. Every hill, every
rock, was a place of danger for the Syrians.

Only a small band of Chasidim opposed a mighty army.
One important decision helped them. They resolved to fight
even on the Sabbath day. Never again would they allow themselves and their children to be helplessly slaughtered.

Mattathias was dying. He had to choose a successor to lead
his fighters. Who would be courageous, strong, and wise?
Whom would the people love and be willing to follow? John,
the oldest, was a good fighter. Jonathan was brave. Eleazar
was impetuous and Simon was wise. But Judah stood out
among all of them. There was no doubt in Mattathias' mind.
Judah, the Maccabee, whose arm was like a mighty hammer,
whose mind was quick and sharp, whose heart was filled with
devotion to his people and his faith—he should be the leader.

Slowly Judah's forces grew. Stories of his strength and his
valor were heard everywhere. Young men came from all over
the land to join forces. Twice, the small band of Judeans defeated a larger Syrian force. The sword of the Syrian general

now hung on Judah's belt, a sign to all of his bold courage.

Judah knew he could never overcome the Syrians by numbers. His strength lay in cunning and strategy. He had to outthink and outsmart the Syrian generals. At Emmaus, he proved that skill could overcome force.

The Syrians were encamped before the plains of Emmaus. Judah and his forces were hidden in the mountains. A battle would soon take place. He called his men together and asked them to fast and pray for strength. Some of the men needed encouragement. "We are so few," they said. Judah replied, "It is no hard matter for many to be handed over to a few, and with the God of Heaven it is all one—to deliver with a great multitude or a small company. Strength cometh from Heaven."

Judah did not wait for the Syrians. His plans were to surprise them. The Syrians started moving toward the Judean forces. They came to the camp. They could not believe their eyes. The camp was empty.

"They must have run away into the mountains," cried the Syrian commander. "Let us follow them."

Where was Judah with his men? No one could possibly guess, for he was in the deserted camp of the Syrians. He had come in from the rear. Unguarded, the camp was now in his hands. Soon it was ablaze, in ruins and flames. All he had to do was to follow the Syrians. By this time they were confused and broken up into small groups. Rushing back and forth from place to place they were an easy prey for the Judeans. Those who could fled from the scene. The rest were overcome. Ammunition, food, and money were the rewards of the battle of Emmaus. More important was the fact that it signaled vic-

tory for Judah and his followers. The Syrian army was shat-
tered. Now Judah could move on with his troops to Jerusalem.
The way was clear. No one opposed him.

Judah, the warrior, was also Judah, the devoted priest. He
entered Jerusalem, determined to throw out all the signs of
idolatry. To clean the Temple filled with symbols of Greek
worship was his first task. The broken walls, the unclean altars, the torn hangings, the ruined vessels, all were either destroyed, hidden away or repaired.

From their hiding places Jews heard the news. They returned to Jerusalem. Everyone helped. In only three weeks
the Temple was in order again. Shining new vessels stood in
their appointed places. Fine hangings decorated the walls;
firm stone altars awaited the sacrifices.

Exactly three years had passed since Antiochus entered the Temple and sacrificed to an idol. On the 25th of Kislev, in the year 165 B.C.E., the Temple was rededicated to the service of God and to the religion for which the Maccabees had fought, which had so nearly been lost.

Judah acted as High Priest. Perhaps he thought of the days of Hezekiah when the Temple was rededicated. That service lasted for eight days. This time the lamps of oil were kindled again for eight days. Judah decreed that every year at the same time, Jews should celebrate their victory by an eight day festival of lights. Chanuko, the festival of rededication, became a part of the Jewish calendar.

SOME QUESTIONS TO ANSWER IN CLASS

What differences were there in the way the Egyptian kings acted toward Judea and the way the Syrian rulers acted?

What holiday commemorates the Maccabean victory?

What were the names of the Maccabean brothers?

How did Judah the Maccabee deserve the name, "fighting priest"?

A TOPIC FOR A DEBATE

The war with the Syrians was more important than any war which the Jewish people had ever fought before.

Choose sides and think up good arguments for your side.

READ

The Unconquered by Gaer
    "Judas the Maccabee," p. 148.
The Lore of the Old Testament by Gaer
    "Daniel and the Lions," p. 301.
The Burning Bush by Gaer
    "The Writing on the Wall," p. 325.
Days and Ways by Gamoran
    "Right against Might," pp. 69–85.

29. INDEPENDENCE

How ANTIOCHUS must have raged to learn that the little ragged band of Judeans, untrained and without arms, had overcome his great army, led by experienced generals! He did not realize that men who fight for money do not fight like men who battle to save their homes, their families, and their faith. Antiochus was coming himself to put down this upstart, this Judah the Maccabee.

In the midst of his planning, however, Antiochus died. For two years Judah was unopposed. To the south, the east, and the north he went with his soldiers. He captured cities which had been taken away by the Edomites and the Ammonites and rescued Jews who had been living among these enemy people. Judah's name was linked to that of David—the warrior king and the warrior priest.

The Syrian general who followed Antiochus on the throne made peace with Judah. All Antiochus' decrees against the Jewish religion were wiped out. Religious freedom was granted. The Chasidim had won. The first great struggle for religious freedom which the world had ever known was successful.

It was not a good peace. The Syrians continued to be political masters of the country. In Jerusalem, they maintained a fortress, manned by Syrian soldiers. This was called the Acra. There were still many Jews in Jerusalem who were opposed to Judah and his followers. To them, Greek customs were most desirable.

In Syria affairs were in a turmoil. A new king was on the throne. He showed his power over Judea by appointing a new High Priest, who also was a follower of Greek ways.

Alcimus, the new High Priest, sent messages to the king against Judah. Before long a huge Syrian army was marching against Judah, led by a famous general named Nicanor. Judah rallied his men and Nicanor was badly defeated. The day of his defeat, the 13th of Ador, became known in Jewish history as Nicanor Day. As you know, Purim, which celebrates another victory, falls on the 14th of Ador.

But the Syrian king had more soldiers and more generals. Once again a vast force came down to crush Judah. He fought a hopeless battle. His army had dwindled away in the face of ceaseless fighting against terrific odds. Many soldiers had gone home when peace was first arranged. Fighting bravely to defend what he had so gloriously won for his people, Judah was killed. The battle was lost.

The leadership of the Maccabean forces fell to Jonathan. Only he and Simon were left of the five brave brothers. There were raids and skirmishes with Syrian soldiers. Then there was a fortunate turn of affairs. The Syrian leaders were busy with political matters. They wanted Judea to be an ally, not an enemy. They made a treaty with Jonathan.

Jonathan became the unofficial ruler of the Jews. Jerusalem was closed to him, but he set up his headquarters in Michmash, an important place in Jewish history. Nine hundred years earlier King Saul had gained his first great victory over the Philistines at Michmash.

Things became better and better. In Syria two parties struggled for the throne. Each one offered Jonathan advantages in return for his loyalty. At last he was able to return to Jerusalem and take over the city. He was named the High Priest. He became the religious and political head of Judea.

What a change took place during the amazing rule of Jonathan! The Syrians, quarreling among themselves, sought his friendship. For help which he gave the king he received the city of Ekron and territory surrounding it. Soon a great part of the seacoast was added to the country. He protected the Temple and fortified the city of Jerusalem with strong, high walls. He set Judea on the road to independence.

The Syrian king who had been friendly to Jonathan was in trouble. One of his generals named Trypho was trying to seize the throne. Jonathan set out to help the king. He commanded a large and well-trained Judean army. To his surprise, the Syrian general did not oppose him. He met Jonathan with gifts and offered to add a new city on the seacoast to Judean

territory. He induced Jonathan to send his forces away and to meet him with only a few men. As soon as he had him in his power, Trypho captured him and treacherously killed him.

Jonathan was a true Maccabee, brave and loyal. The country mourned him.

In 142 B.C.E. the last Maccabean brother was called on to lead the people of Judea. This was Simon, a wise, just man. An assembly of the priests and elders of the people met in Jerusalem. They chose Simon to be their ruler. He was given the title of High Priest, Commander of the Army and Prince of the Nation.

Simon, too, won many advantages from the Syrians. He finally besieged the fortress at Jerusalem. The last of the Hellenists left the fortress. It became a stronghold to guard Jerusalem and a place for soldiers to live.

At last the Syrians were out of the country. Judea was really free! As a sign of independence, Simon had coins minted, the very first Judean coins ever made. He had a strong army at his command and he received the love and loyalty of the people.

The Maccabean war began as a struggle for religious freedom. When it ended, twenty-five years later, much more had been won. For the first time in almost six hundred years Judea did not have to pay tribute or taxes to another country. It was a free and independent state. Mattathias and his sons had done better than they dreamed.

They had proved that might does not make right. They had shown that the fires of liberty and religious freedom could not be quenched. Their struggle had saved the ancient Hebrew ideals of the Bible. They had proved the inner strength of Judaism. The Jewish people would not give up the customs, laws, and ideals which made up their traditions for another way of life.

Judaism continued to be a living force, so strong that in time it became the mother of two other religions, Christianity and Mohammedanism. These would become larger in numbers, but would always be in debt to their parent religion for their basic ideas and thoughts. In this way, the greater part of the world owes its religious faith to that small band of fighters, the Maccabees.

QUESTIONS TO ANSWER

What two victories are celebrated on days following each other? On the 13th of Ador? On the 14th of Ador?

What titles did the last Maccabean brother receive?

In what special way did he show that Judea was independent?

What were the rewards of the Maccabean victory?

SOMETHING TO DO

Write a composition or a poem with the title, "A Brave Family" or "In the Footsteps of Their Father." You may think of another title that you like better.

CHILDREN'S READING LIST

BAITY, ELIZABETH CHESLEY, *Man Is a Weaver*, Viking Press.

BARNES, FRANKLIN, *Man and His Records*, Follett Pub. Co. (Out of print).

BELTH, NORMAN (Ed.), *The World Over Story Book*, Bloch Publishing Co.

The Bible, Jewish Publication Society.

BILDERSEE, ADELE, *Out of the House of Bondage*, Union of American Hebrew Congregations.

———, *The Story of Genesis*, UAHC.*

BONSER, EDNA M., *How the Early Hebrews Lived and Learned*, The Macmillan Co.

Central Conference of American Rabbis, *Union Prayerbook* (Newly Revised).

EDIDIN, BEN M., *Rebuilding Palestine*, Behrman House, Inc.

EISENBERG, AZRIEL (Ed.), *The Bar Mitzvah Treasury*, Behrman.

ESSRIG AND SEGAL, *Israel Today*, UAHC.

FINE, HELEN, *Behold, the Land*, UAHC.

FREEHOF, LILLIAN S., *Second Bible Legend Book*, UAHC.

———, *Stories of King David*, J.P.S.**

FREUND, MIRIAM K., *Jewels for a Crown*, McGraw-Hill.

GAER, JOSEPH, *The Burning Bush*, UAHC.

———, *The Lore of the Old Testament*, Little Brown & Co.

———, *The Unconquered*, UAHC.

GAMORAN, MAMIE G., *Days and Ways*, UAHC.

———, *Hillel's Happy Holidays*, UAHC.

———, *The Voice of the Prophets*, UAHC.

———, *With Singer and Sage*, UAHC.

GOLUB, ROSE W., *Down Holiday Lane*, UAHC.

The Jewish Encyclopedia, Isidore Singer (Ed.), Funk and Wagnalls Co.

* *Union of American Hebrew Congregations*
** *Jewish Publication Society*

241

JONES, ELIZABETH ORTON, *David*, The Macmillan Co.

LANDMAN, ISAAC, *Stories of the Prophets*, UAHC.

LEVIN, MEYER, *If I Forget Thee*, Viking Press.

LEVINGER, ELMA E., *Great Jewish Women*, Behrman House, Inc.

LURIE, ROSE G., *The Great March*, Book I, UAHC.

PESSIN, DEBORAH, *The Aleph-Bet Story Book*, J.P.S.

SCHWARZ, JACOB D., *In the Land of Kings and Prophets*, UAHC.

———, *Into the Promised Land*, UAHC.

SMITHER, ETHEL L., *A Picture Book of Palestine*, Abingdon-Cokesbury Press.

TUBBY, RUTH P., *A Picture Dictionary of the Bible*, Abingdon-Cokesbury Press.

Universal Jewish Encyclopedia, Isaac Landman (Ed.), Universal Jewish Encyclopedia, Inc.

WHITE, ANNE TERRY, *Lost Worlds*, Random House.

TEACHER'S BIBLIOGRAPHY

The Apocrypha

The Bible, Jewish Publication Society.

BURROWS, MILLAR, *What Mean These Stones?* American School of Oriental Research.

Central Conference of American Rabbis, *Union Hymnal.*

————, *Union Prayerbook* (Newly Revised).

COOPERSMITH, HARRY, *The Songs We Sing*, United Synagogue.

FINKELSTEIN, LOUIS (Ed.), *The Jews*, J.P.S.*

FREEHOF, SOLOMON B., *The Book of Psalms*, Union of American Hebrew Congregations.

————, *Preface to Scripture*, UAHC.**

GLUECK, NELSON, *The Other Side of the Jordan*, American School of Oriental Research.

GRAYZEL, SOLOMON, *A History of the Jews*, J.P.S.

MARGOLIS, MAX L. and ALEXANDER MARX, *A History of the Jewish People*, J.P.S.

MILLER, MADELINE S. and J. LANE MILLER, *Encyclopedia of Bible Life*, Harper and Brothers.

ORLINSKY, HARRY M., *Israel in the Ancient Near East.*

PESSIN, DEBORAH and TEMIMA GEZARI, *The Jewish Kindergarten*, UAHC.

RADIN, MAX, *Life of the People in Bible Times*, J.P.S.

TREPP, LEO, *Eternal Faith, Eternal People*, Prentice-Hall, Inc.

WRIGHT, G. F. and F. V. FILSON, *Historical Atlas to the Bible*, Westminster Press.

  * *Jewish Publication Society*
  ** *Union of American Hebrew Congregations*

Pronouncing List

Ahab—Ā'-hăb
Ahaz—Ā'-hăz
Ahijah—Ă-hē'-jȧ
Akhnaton—Ăk'-nä-tŏn
Amaziah—Ăm-ȧ-zī'-ȧ
Anathoth—Ă'-nȧ-tŏth
Anshei K'neses Ha-g'dolo—Ăn-shā
   K'nĕ'-sĕs Hä-g'dō'-lô
Antiochus—Ăn-tī'-ŏ-kŭs
Apocrypha—Ȧ-pŏk'-rĭ-fȧ
Athaliah—Ă-thă-lī'-ȧ
Baal—Bā'-ăl
Beer-sheba—Bĕr-shē'-vȧ
Canaan—Kā'-năn
Canaanites—Kā'-nȧ-nītes
Chasidim—Chä-sē'-dĕm
Darius—Dȧ-rī'-ŭs
Edomites—Ĕ'-dō-mītes
Eleazar—Ĕl-lē-ā'-zär
Eli—Ē'-lī
Elijah—Ē-lī'-jȧ
Elisha—Ē-lī'-shȧ
Ephraim—Ē'-frā-ĭm
Euphrates—Ū̇-frā'-tēs
Gedaliah—Gĕ-däl'-yȧ
Hadad—Hä-däd'
Haran—Hä-rän'
Hezekiah—Hĕ-zĕ-kī'-ȧ
Hosea—Hō-zā'-ȧ
Hoshea—Hō-shē'-ȧ
Huldah—Hŭl'-dȧ

Isaiah—Ī-zā'-yȧ
Issachar—Ĭs'-ȧ-kär
Jabesh-gilead—Jā'-bĕsh-gĭl'-ē-ăd
Jebusites—Jĕb'-ù-sītes
Jehoiachin—Jĕ-hoi'-ȧ-kĭn
Jehoiadah—Jĕ-hoi'-ȧ-dä
Jehoram—Jĕ-hō'-răm
Jehoshaphat—Jĕ-hōsh'-ȧ-făt
Jehu—Jā'-hū
Jezreel—Jĕz'-rĕ-ĕl
Kadesh Barnea—Kä'-dĕsh Bär-nā'-ȧ
Levi—Lē'-vī
Machpelah—Mäch-pĕ'-lȧ
Malachi—Măl'-ȧ-kī
Mamre—Măm'-rä
Mattathias—Mă-tă-thī'-ăs
Menahem—Mĕn'-ȧ-hĕm
Menelaus—Mĕn-ĕ-lā'-ŭs
Naboth—Nā'-bŏth
Nahum—Nā'-hŭm
Nebuchadnezzar—Nĕb-ù-käd-nĕt'-sär
Nehemiah—Nĕ-hĕ-mī'-ȧ
Nicanor—Nĭ-kä'-nŏr
Omri—Ŏm'-rē
Ptolemy—Tŏl'-ĕ-mē
Ramah—Rä'-mä
Seleucus—Sĕ-lū'-kŭs
Sennacherib—Sĕ-năk'-ĕ-rĭb
Shechem—Shĕ-chĕm'
Shiloh—Shī'-lō
Siloam—Sĭ-lō'-ăm

Simeon—Sĭm'-ē-ŏn
Tabor—Tā'-bôr
Tekoa—Tĕ-kō'-à
Ur of Chaldees—Ūr of Kăl'-dēs
Xerxes—Zérk'-sēs
Yam Chinnereth—Yäm Kĭ-nĕr'-ĕth

Zebulun—Zĕb'-û-lŭn
Zechariah—Zĕ-kă-rī'-à
Zedekiah—Zĕ-dĕ-kī'-à
Zephaniah—Zĕ-fă-nī'-à
Zerubbabel—Zĕ-rū'-bă-bĕl

INDEX

A

Aaron, 34, 44, 65, 93
Abraham, 3, 5, 11, 14, 19, 23, 63, 65
Acra, 237
Ahab, 116–117, 129–133
Ahaz, 145, 162
Ahijah, 103, 121
Akhnaton, 28
Alexander the Great, 219–220
Alexandria, 216, 220–221
Amalekites, 83
Amaziah the priest, 141
Ammon, 56
Ammonites, 73–74, 92, 104, 236
Amorites, 46, 63
Amos, 120, 141–143
Anathoth, 179
Anshei K'neses Ha-g'dolo, 215
Antioch, 220, 229
Antiochus IV, 229, 236
Apocrypha, 214–215
Arabs, 19
Aram, 12, 92, 111, 117, 133, 137, 145
Aramaic, 202
Archeologists, 9–11
Archeology, 60
Ark of the Covenant, 44, 65, 78, 92, 100
Ashdod, 74, 92, 167
Asher, tribe of, 68
Assyria, 56, 124, 142, 144–145, 162, 168, 177, 189
Athaliah, 117, 134

B

Baal, 71, 117, 135
Babylonia, 14, 56, 168, 177, 181, 189; life of exiles in, 189–190, 202
Barak, 69–70
Bashan, people of, 46
Beer-sheba, 53
Benjamin, tribe of, 69, 111
Bethel, 61, 112, 137–139, 176
Bethlehem, 87
Bible, 8, 19, 195, 213, 221

C

Canaan, 9, 12, 14, 17, 24, 45, 49, 64; geography of, 51–57
Canaanites, 68, 104
Canon, 213
Chanuko, 235
Chasidim, 227, 229–230, 232
Christianity, 240
Cyrus, 193, 195

D

Damascus, 92, 103, 117, 133, 137, 145
Dan, city of, 53, 112; tribe of, 74
Daniel, Book of, 230–231
Darius, 200
David, 86–98, 104, 110
Dead Sea (Salt Sea), 54
Deborah, 67–71; Song of, 70
Deuteronomy, Book of, 173–175, 177

E

Edomites, 83, 92, 102, 236
Egypt, 9, 12, 14, 21, 24–26, 112, 124, 137, 145, 166, 180, 183, 185; Jews living there, 216, 221
Egyptians, idea of God, 28; skills of, 27, 28
Ekron, 74, 238
ELEAZAR THE MACCABEE, 232
ELI, 78–79
ELIJAH, 5, 117, 121, 129, 131–132
ELISHA, 121, 131–133
Ephraim, tribe of, 63, 68–69, 73, 109
ESAU, 23–24
Euphrates, 12
Exodus, Book of, 173; from Egypt, 35
EZEKIEL, 191–192
EZRA, 202–204, 206–207

F

Fertile Crescent, 12–14, 51

G

Gad, tribe of, 46–47, 56, 68, 73
Galilee, Sea of, 12, 54
Gath, 74, 169
Gaza, 74, 89
GEDALIAH, 185
Gibeah, 81–83, 85
Gibeon, 61–63, 104
Gibeonites, 61–63, 104
GIDEON, 71–73
Gilead, 56, 73–74, 81
GOD, Abraham's idea of, 17; Egyptian idea, 28; Greek idea, 224–225; Moses' idea, 34, 42; nomad idea, 16; Pharaoh's idea, 26; prophets' idea, 123–125
GOLIATH, 86–88
Goshen, 26, 31
Great Assembly, 215

Greek ideas and learning, 220, 224–225; translation of Pentateuch, 223

H

HADAD, 102
HAGGAI, 199
Haran, 15, 17, 23
Hebrew(s), 14, 21, 25, 28, 42–43
Hellenism, 226–228, 239
Hellenists, 226–228, 239
HEZEKIAH, 160–162, 167–168
High Priest, 209–211, 221, 227, 237
HIRAM, 99, 104
Holy of Holies, 100, 227
HOSEA, 142
HOSHEA, 145
HULDAH, 174

I

Idols, 16, 19, 105, 117
Idol-Worship, 68, 123, 158, 163–164, 173, 227
Iron, production of, 94
ISAAC, 15, 19, 23
ISAIAH, 161–169
ISAIAH THE SECOND, 193–194
Israel, new state of, 8, 54
Israel, kingdom of, 111, 114–117, 144–148
Israelites, 64, 69, 75
ISSACHAR, 63, 68–69

J

Jabesh-gilead, 81–82, 90
JACOB, 15, 19, 24–26
Jebusites, 91
JEHOIACHIN, 190, 198
JEHOIADA, 134–135
JEHORAM, 117
JEHOSHAPHAT, 114
JEHU, 132–133
JEPHTHAH, 73, 81

JEREMIAH, 172, 179–185, 191, 200
Jericho, 54, 59–60
JEROBOAM, 103, 109, 111
JEROBOAM II, 135, 137–138, 143
Jerusalem, 55, 64, 91–93, 96, 152–158, 164–165, 238
JETHRO, 33–34, 70
JEZEBEL, 117, 123, 130, 132–134
Jezreel, Valley of, 14, 55
JOASH, 134
JOHN THE MACCABEE, 232
JONATHAN, 82–83, 85, 88–90, 95
JONATHAN THE MACCABEE, 232, 237–239
Jordan River, 14, 17, 46–47, 54, 73
JOSEPH, 5, 25, 38
JOSHUA, 45–46, 59–66, 78, 93
JOSHUA, priest of Judeans, 198–199
JOSIAH, 171–177
JOTHAM, 135
Judah, kingdom of, 111, 114, 133–135, 151–158, 162, 185–186; tribe of, 68, 74, 91, 111
JUDAH THE MACCABEE, 232–237
Judea, life in, 197, 202–203, 209–216
Judges, 40, 67–74, 77, 153

K

Kadesh Barnea, 45–46
Kings, First Book of, 101
Kishon River, 55, 70
Koheleth, 101

L

Lamentations, 184–185
Levi, tribe of, 65
Levites, 100, 156, 211
Lost Ten Tribes, 146–147
LOT, 15, 18

M

Maccabees, 231–240

Machpelah, cave of, 19, 23, 26
MALACHI, 210
Mamre, 19
MANASSEH, KING, 171
Manasseh, tribe of, 46–47, 56, 63, 68, 71, 73
MATTATHIAS, 231–232
Mediterranean Sea, 55, 74, 94
MENAHEM, 144
MENELAUS, 227, 230
Mesopotamia, 9, 12, 14
MICAH, 169–170
Michmash, 83, 237
Midianites, 71, 99
Midrash, 215
Mizpah, 78, 81, 185
Moab, 48, 56, 115, 137
Moabites, 92, 103
Modin, 231
Mohammedanism, 240
MOSES, 32–48, 65, 78, 93, 120, 173
Mt. Carmel, 55
Mt. Gilboa, 89
Mt. Moriah, 112
Mt. Sinai, 40
Mt. Tabor, 69–70

N

NABOTH, 130–131
NAHUM, 172, 176
Naphtali, tribe of, 63, 69
NATHAN, 98
NEBUCHADNEZZAR, 181, 183–185
NEHEMIAH, 202, 204–207, 214
NICANOR, 237
Nile, 12, 24
Nineveh, 168, 171, 176

O

OMRI, 115–116

P

Palestine, 8, 53
Passover, 45, 129, 176

PEKAH, 144–145
Persia, 195, 209, 216
PHARAOH, 25, 34; as a god, 26
Philistines, 74, 78, 82–83, 86–94
Phoenicia, 94, 137
Phoenicians, 27, 98–99, 115, 117
Priests, 65, 100, 155–156
Prophecy, books of, 123
Prophets, 107, 120–125; early, 120, 132; literary (later), 120, 123; schools of, 120–121
Proverbs, Book of, 101
Psalms, Book of, 95–96, 200–201
PTOLEMY (ies), 220, 221
Purim, 216, 237

Q
QUEEN OF SHEBA, 101

R
Ramah, 79
Red Sea, 36
REHOBOAM, 106, 109–112
Reuben, tribe of, 46–47, 56, 68, 73
Ruth, Book of, 204

S
Samaria, 116, 133, 137, 145
Samaritans, 147, 198–199, 207, 213
SAMUEL, 79–80, 86–87, 103–104, 121–122
SAUL, 80–91, 95, 110, 122, 238
Schools, 156
Scribes, 156, 212
Sea of Reeds, 36
SELEUCUS, 220
SENNACHERIB, 168
Shechem, 24, 109, 111
Shiloh, 65, 68, 72, 78–79
Siloam, 160
Simeon, tribe of, 68
SIMON THE JUST, 221

SIMON THE MACCABEE, 232, 237, 239
SISERA, 69–70
Slavery, 31–32, 38, 225–226
Slaves, 31, 154, 174, 206, 225–226
SOLOMON, 97–106, 110, 137
Song of Songs, 101
Syria, 219–220, 224, 231–232
Syrians, 219–220, 224, 231–232

T
Tabernacle, 44
Tekoa, 141–142
Temple of Solomon, 98–100, 105; cleansed and rededicated by Maccabees, 233–234; rebuilt by Judeans, 198–201; Hezekiah's rededication of, 168
Ten Commandments, 41–42, 47, 66, 173
Tent of Meeting, 44, 65
Theocracy, 202
Tigris, 12
Twelve tribes, 29
Tyre, 98–99, 104

U
United Nations, 8
Ur of Chaldees, 15–16
UZZIAH, 135, 162

X
XERXES, 201

Y
Yam Kinereth, 54

Z
Zebulun, tribe of, 63, 69
ZECHARIAH, 200
ZEDEKIAH, 182
ZEPHANIAH, 172
ZERUBBABEL, 198–199, 201
Zion, 92–93

UNION GRADED SERIES

EDITED BY

EMANUEL GAMORAN, PH.D., *Director of Education*
Union of American Hebrew Congregations